authentic recipes from
morocco

60 Simple and Delicious Recipes
from the Land of the Tagine

Recipes and text by **Fatema Hal**
Photographs by **Jean-François Hamon** and
Bruno Barbey
Styling by **Daniele Schnapp**

PERIPLUS EDITIONS
Singapore • Hong Kong • Indonesia

Published by Periplus Editions with editorial offices at
61 Tai Seng Avenue #02-12, Singapore 534167

Hardcover ISBN-10: 0-7946-0325-4
          ISBN-13: 978-0-7946-0325-0

Distributed by

North America, Latin America and Europe
Tuttle Publishing, 364 Innovation Drive
North Clarendon, VT 05759-9436 U.S.A.
Tel: 1 (802) 773-8930; Fax: 1 (802) 773-6993
info@tuttlepublishing.com
www.tuttlepublishing.com

Japan
Tuttle Publishing, Yaekari Building, 3rd Floor
5-4-12 Osaki; Shinagawa-ku; Tokyo 141 0032
Tel: (81) 03 5437-0171; Fax: (81) 03 5437-0755
tuttle-sales@gol.com

Asia Pacific
Berkeley Books Pte Ltd.
61 Tai Seng Avenue #02-12, Singapore 534167
Tel: (65) 6280-1330; Fax: (65) 6280-6290
inquiries@periplus.com.sg
www.periplus.com

Photo Credits
All food and location photography by Jean-François
Hamon. Additional photos by La Maison Arabe
(Thierry Laureut), p. 11; Magnum Photos (Bruno
Barbey), pp. 5, 6, 8–9, 14, 15, 17, 18–19, 20, 22–23,
24, 25 and 26.

Acknowledgements
The publisher wishes to thank the following for their
generous assistance: Mr Ho Cheow Teck, Honorary
Consul, Consulate of the Kingdom of Morocco,
Singapore; Björn Conerding's, Ursula Haldimann,
and Enija Luna of Riad Enija; Mohamed Harda
(hôtel Le Littoral), N'guyer Hj Mustapha B. Hj Omar
(Marrakesh), Liwan, Siécle, Médina, Terre de Sable,
Raynaud, Christofle, Baya, Mokuba, Colline des
Potiers, Fee d'Herbe; Monete Aline, Stéphanie
Bertrand, Sandrine Duviller, Joël Puentes, Fabrizion
Ruspoli (La Maison Arabe), and Samuel Rodany.

Printed in Singapore

10 09 08 07
5 4 3 2 1

Contents

Food in Morocco

Moroccan cuisine has been nurtured by centuries of Mediterranean influence

The history of Morocco has always been closely intertwined with the history of the Mediterranean. As a veritable crossroads of civilizations—an asylum for the Andalousian Jews and Arabs who were chased out of the kingdom of Grenada at the end of the 15th century; later a French Protectorate until its independence in 1956—Morocco offers an exceptional example of generosity and harmony. This multifaceted country reflects diverse regional, ethnic, and social influences, all of which left their mark on its past. It is this variety that gives Moroccan cuisine its unparalleled reputation. Moroccan cuisine is considered to be one the finest in the world and some of its most celebrated dishes have justly taken their place among the culinary classics of the world.

The "Isle of the Sunset," *Djerirat-al-Maghrib* as the first Arab geographers named the land that would become Morocco, offers the traveler very diverse landscapes. First, there is the Atlantic Ocean lapping the shores in the west; then there are the Atlas and Rif Mountains that enclose a vast amphitheater reaching from the southwest to the northwest of Morocco; further south, the immense deserts that are still inhabited by nomadic peoples; and finally the central regions that spill out to the ocean where alternating plateaus, plains, and valleys have favored the development of culture and the rise of great cities.

The first inhabitants of Morocco were the Berbers who were invaded by the Omeyyad Arab dynasty of conquering warriors. Their empire reached from the Indus to the shores of northwest Africa. They built Muslim Spain and created a great civilization that reigned over the southern half of the peninsula and over Andalousia in particular.

In the eleventh and twelfth centuries, the Almoravid dynasty of Berbers, followed by the Almohad Berber dynasty, succeeded the Omeyyads as rulers of the Muslim territories in North Africa and Spain, and were responsible for the unification of Morocco.

Sub-Saharan Africa also left its mark on Morocco, trad-ing its gold and other riches: the caravans that converged on the North included large numbers of women from Mali or the Sudan who would become the peerless *dadas*, the cooks who hold the secrets to the Moroccan kitchen.

It is this social and geographical diversity, and the peaceful cohabitation of different ethnic groups, that has enabled such a fine cuisine to evolve.

From north to south, Morocco offers travelers a wealth of contrasting landscapes. From the harsh winters of the Rif Mountains to the blazing caress of the Sahara, each region has developed its own ways with food, even if there are many elements that are shared from one province to the next. *Mechoui* (barbecued lamb) or *kessra* (bread) may be found in every region of the kingdom but the recipes have been adapted to suit the conditions in which they are made.

Take couscous—the national dish—for example. In the countryside, the ruggedness of everyday life imposes a sense of humility in the preparation of the dish: dried fava beans replace garbanzo beans while dried meat (*gueddid*) replaces the more tender, subtle, and more expensive fresh lamb.

The coastal regions have developed their own original couscous called *kasksou baddaz*, in which dried sweet corn replaces the traditional semolina and fish from the Mediterranean or Atlantic enriches the dish.

Austere desert life also contributes its own touch. In the regions where man must often content himself with a few dates and a little milk, couscous is accompanied by small fresh dates (*kuran*) that are baked until almost candied. There are even varieties of couscous made from barley or rice, again reflecting the heritage of the *dadas*.

ABOVE: This shop in the Aït Ourir *souk* (market) east of Marrakech offers tagines cooked over *kanounes*, a kind of clay cauldron.
OPPOSITE: An impressive spread of tasty Moroccan snacks and appetizers.

In the furthermost regions, meat is rare and dishes are invariably flavored with spices. Here, visual appearance is paramount. All the senses are called upon to appreciate these attractive dishes with their heady aromas. Cooks are as skilled in marrying tastes as they are in assembling colors.

The result is a cuisine that is festive and sensual. Some claim it even possesses medicinal qualities. Arab doctors have always made use of certain foods to cure their patients, without losing sight of the question of taste. One of them, Al-Rasi, hit upon the idea of coating medicinal decoctions in sugar to make the remedy more pleasant.

Religion has also played its part in shaping the eating habits of the Moroccan people. Religious directives addressed the issue of food early on and certain restrictions came into force. Pork is forbidden, as is any animal that has not been sacrificed in a religious rite—Jews refer to this sanctified meat as "kosher," Muslims call it "halal." Despite their solemnity, religious celebrations are also at the root of a number of original recipes that are served at specific times of the year. For example, it is with harira that the fast imposed by the month of Ramadan is broken every evening. This soup, both delicious and nourishing, soothes the hunger of the day and brings members of the family together. On these evenings, and much to the delight of the children present, pastries such as grioch, shebbakiya, selou, and sfenji are also served.

It is in the great imperial cities that the Moroccan art de vivre reaches its zenith. Note the words of a civil servant from the finance ministry in 1885: "Thus at last, Great Chamberlain, will the preparations to welcome the Sultan be concluded. No fewer than thirty-three dishes will follow: salads, couscous, pastilla, tagine of poultry, meat, fish [...]. Scoundrels from backwater provinces will be left speechless before such abundance and magnificence and they will admire with near religious devotion the white bread served for the occasion."

Large meals, or diffa, follow an immutable ritual: salads are served one after the other and then make way for the famous pastilla (pie) of pigeon. This is followed by mechoui (barbecued lamb), various tagines, couscous, and, finally, mouthwatering pastries.

A flask of scented water is always passed among guests so they may wash their hands and rinse their palates. Finally, guests enjoy a glass of mint tea, the gratifying conclusion to any great diffa worthy of the name.

Opening the doors to Morocco, we enter a world of tastes and colors that reveal great richness and incomparable skills. In doing so, we perpetuate an authentic tradition, a refined and unequaled celebration of the senses.

ABOVE: The symbol of Marrakech and of Morocco as a whole, Jemaà el Fna Square bustles every evening with food stalls selling skewered meat, soups, snails, and much more. Jugglers, fire-eaters, snake charmers, storytellers, and monkey trainers add to the nightly spectacle.
RIGHT: Mint tea, Morocco's national drink.

The Riches of a Generous Past

Morocco's sumptuous history of cooking has placed the country on the world's culinary stage.

History has rarely provided a better example of people living in such effortless communion than medieval Andalousia. Back then, Christians, Jews, and Muslims shared the same lands and the same way of life. Each group developed its own faith, and art rose to the heights of grace. O blessed Andalousia, for a time the Mediterranean blew a wind of peace onto your shores. But at the end of the fifteenth century, this peace was irrevocably shattered when the Catholic kings from the north broke the truce and forced the Jews and Muslims to choose between conversion or exile.

Banished from Spain, some took refuge in North Africa, perpetuating their long tradition of peaceful cohabitation. Their food, music, and dress were very similar. Admittedly, in the kasbah of Algiers or in the alleyways of Marrakech, the Jews had separate quarters reserved for them, but everyone lived together on good terms. With their shared history, it is difficult today to unravel the bonds that unite Jews and Muslims. As a reflection of this history, Moroccan cuisine is a veritable lesson in sharing, curiosity, generosity, and harmony.

The regional cuisine of the Berbers was already in existence when the Muslim Arabs arrived. Later, the *dadas* (female slaves) from Bilad Al-Sudan and the Jews who were banished from Spain each, in turn, enriched the culinary art of Morocco. Despite them living in close quarters and accumulating culinary skills, many dishes retained their uniqueness.

I remember that my mother adored eating *rkak* (matzo, unleavened bread) that our Jewish neighbor made. Whenever our neighbor could, she would give some to my mother, who would offer her own homemade bread in return. As they enjoyed each other's breads, they traded their baking secrets. But since neither was ever completely successful in making the other's recipe, they continued to exchange their breads as they had before. Our table was rich and varied with Jewish cuisine distinguishing itself through its pastries and the subtlety of its breads.

Unlike in other regions where Ottoman occupation resulted in the disappearance of local culinary traditions, Moroccan cooking was gently imbued with the influences of foreign cuisines. The exiles who arrived from Grenada were warmly welcomed and, in the same vein, African slaves from the south were generally treated well.

No border is impenetrable. At the northeastern tip of Morocco, the town of Oujda faces that of Tlemcen, in Algeria. For centuries, travelers crossed the border in both directions carrying with them their foods and culinary skills—their invisible heritage—thus rendering the exact origins of many dishes impossible to determine.

Despite the difficulties in tracing the culinary history of Morocco, there is one unwavering fact: only the cooking of the ancient communities has found a place and made a lasting impression among the peoples it encountered. In the nineteenth century, Europeans imported new utensils and products but their influence is only very recent because their interaction with the locals was limited to purely administrative affairs.

In an Algerian novel, a *fellah* (or farmhand) recalls how he had never seen sugar as white as that brought by American soldiers during World War II. At the time, such a product was only available on the black market. It was only in the 1970s that French cuisine took hold here, with hors d'œuvres, sweets, and remarkable pastries. The bakeries that made round bread saw production drop in favor of carefully calibrated baguettes. Even the *sfenjis*—fritters sold on the streets which children delighted in—have been supplanted.

As in many countries where cooking benefits from the privilege of tradition, good restaurants are rare in Morocco. If a traveler is not invited to the table in a private home, he will leave with an indifferent impression of Moroccan cuisine. Large hotels prefer to serve indefinable international cuisine to please the masses, rather than offer traditional fare that might upset the undiscriminating tourist. And that is how the gourmet could miss the roads that lead to the delicate flavors of a pigeon *pastilla* or a patiently simmered tagine of apricots and pine nuts. Unless, that is, he meets a Moroccan family who will take it upon themselves to defend the culinary honor of their country.

ABOVE: Porters from Telouet carrying couscous and bread to a *diffa* (*banquet*).
RIGHT: The dining room of a traditional restaurant looking onto a patio planted with orange trees.
PREVIOUS PAGE: The valley of Tinerhir, east of the High Atlas Mountains.

Moroccan cuisine is in fact family cooking. It demands the communion of family members for the traditional dinner at home or, less frequently, for a wedding, a birth, or a baptism. Each family adds its own personal touch, some jealously guarded secret only handed down from mother to daughter. The art requires both skill and memory. Most older Moroccan women are not familiar with the written word. Morocco belongs to a civilization where giving one's word is worth more than a piece of paper, where speaking is a surer signature than can be made with the ink of a pen.

So we run the risk of seeing dishes that formerly enjoyed widespread admiration disappear. Tastes change, as do methods of cooking and conservation. Time works faster than a thoroughbred from the royal stables; the *dadas* are disappearing, and with them, their vast culinary knowledge.

The dominant roles played by Europe and the United States in today's world arena greatly influences the way of life in the other continents. If traditional Moroccan fare is not often found in restaurants in Morocco, it is because when Moroccans go out today, they are seeking food that is new and different.

Today, rice is part of the diet in many Moroccan households, and ketchup and Coca-Cola also have their place on the kitchen table. In some places, *pastilla* is even garnished with Chinese noodles!

It is pointless to remain closed to all foreign influences—

an impossible feat anyway in the face of the unstoppable progression of globalization—but changes should be made with respect for the balance of a dish to prevent it becoming an ungainly amalgam of incompatible parts.

Apart from a few notable exceptions, it is comparatively difficult to find a large number of good Moroccan restaurants within the country. Paradoxically, the situation is quite different abroad. In the United States, France, Britain, and throughout the world, there are many excellent eateries that, for the most part, respect the Moroccan culinary traditions. Moroccan cuisine is, without doubt, a good export.

However, it would be a mistake to claim that one must travel outside Morocco to enjoy traditional Moroccan food. The Moroccans are noted for their hospitality, so do accept all invitations to visit Moroccan homes, join the inhabitants at their kitchen tables, and share in their simple, subtle, and very tasty recipes.

ABOVE: Out of respect for bread, it must not be touched by a knife, which would be considered an act of violence. Bread should be broken. Food that has been given by God and blessed in His name before the meal should not be degraded by such an instrument.

Women and Dadas
Moroccan cuisine is essentially a feminine art

In Morocco, cuisine is first and foremost women's business. In Moroccan culture, men are strongly advised to stay away from ovens, or risk losing their virility.

Morocco is a country of oral tradition, even though progress and education are gradually reaching across the immense territory. Here, knowledge, culinary or otherwise, is dispensed by word of mouth, from mother to daughter. So, should you be invited into a Moroccan home and the mistress of the house allows you free reign after the indispensable mint tea ceremony, you will not see any books on the subject of food and you will certainly not find any recipe books.

We have seen that Morocco is rich in its varied populations. The Berbers were the first inhabitants. Several ethnological studies have shown that Berber women worked the land, harvested, picked, and did the cooking themselves. Clearly our culinary roots go back to cultures from pre-Islamic times (North Africa was the larder of the Roman Empire) and can be traced to local savoir faire. Since that time, Morocco has had close commercial ties with countries in the south of the continent; sub-Saharan Africa provided gold, salt, and slaves. Trade reached its height under the green banner of Islam and became a flourishing commerce that affected the whole society including the cuisine.

Brutal import of servant populations was quickly replaced by peaceful solutions, and it was usually through trade that abundant supplies of slaves were sent to the market of Dâr al-Islam, the house of Islam. In Morocco, male and female slaves came primarily from Sudan. Many had been bought by Touareg traders for a few pieces of gold and some scraps of fabric; others had simply been rounded up on the banks of the Niger. They instructed the captives in the rudiments of Arabic and the principles of Islam (which increased their market value) before leading them to Moroccan markets where they were sold.

ABOVE: Desert-dwelling nomad women prepare couscous, the national dish of Morocco.

We do not know much about the living conditions of the first sub-Saharan African slaves. Observers conclude that, at least after the nineteenth century, they did not suffer at the hands of their employers. The masters even tended to be more humane with sub-Saharan African slaves because though originally pagan, they quickly chose to convert to Islam.

Female slaves, known as *dadas*, quickly became indispensable, and were even given the charge of young children, for whom their *dadas* remain an indelible memory. Bound to slavery during the lifetime of their masters, some of the *dadas* stayed on in the house of the heirs when the latter died, to continue doing what they did as slaves, though henceforth as free women.

Almost all female slaves were destined to perform domestic tasks. However, through the attention of a merchant or a rich master, a few, thought to be good learners, received a thorough education in music or even literature, before being sent to the harems of many an Orientalist's fancy.

Qualified cooks were sold for very large sums. Restrictive and strict regulations were set so that the cooks' instruction conformed to the wishes of the palace. Over the course of several years, the cooks were fed, housed, and trained until they perfected their knowledge and skill. The training period was crowned by a sort of diploma, a certificate with the slave's name and her culi-

nary aptitudes. It comes as no surprise that these slaves commanded such high prices.

Other than the original contributions from Berber culture, Moroccan cuisine is largely made up of the heritage of the *dadas* whose numbers are now dwindling. The height of irony is that these women whose only wealth was their status as a slave have become the masters of an inestimable, delectable treasure. When a *dada* is no more, a whole chapter of our culinary heritage is lost. To borrow the words of African writer Hampaté Bâ: "When one of them passes away, it is a library burning." It has become urgent to record all the recipes and kitchen hints of these women in order to preserve their memories, which have been jealously guarded in household kitchens.

Heiresses to an ancient knowledge, these women have acquired real power in the home. It has been one of the only means at their disposal to demonstrate their competence and the hours they have spent tending their ovens may soon be lost forever, as will a part of our culinary memory.

ABOVE: Mouloud, one of the most important Muslim holidays, celebrates the birth of the prophet Mohammed. It is marked by processions, dancing, and feasts.
RIGHT: The great tradition of street food is perpetuated by the women of Morocco.

Grand Imperial Cuisine

The art and splendor of Moroccan cooking is found in the fabled cities
of Rabat, Fes, Meknes and Marrakech.

Since the seventeenth century, no fewer than four imperial cities have laid claim to being the capital of the sherifan empire of Morocco. Rabat, Fes, Meknes, and Marrakech are all names that ring out as splendors of the past. Each was the capital in its time and they have never ceased being rivals. All have laid claim to their own styles of architecture, music and, of course, cooking.

Marrakech was founded in the eleventh century by Berber horsemen from southern Morocco, under the leadership of Youssef Ibn Tachfine who established the Almoravid dynasty, before being conquered by the Almohad sultan Abd al-Mumin in AD 1147. The city first owed its fame to the fact that it was on the trade route from Timbuktu to the north, used by caravans laden with spices and gold coins. Today, the cuisine of Marrakech is notably rich and is a reminder of those luxurious times of old. It is a somewhat ostentatious fare that is presented to foreigners who flow through the gates of city.

The souks (markets) are unforgettable. They are bursting with spices and you can still purchase real *ras el hanout*, the fabulous alchemy of twenty-seven spices that is almost impossible to find today. It is also the city of *tanjia marrakshia*, a dish initially served only to unmarried men, which has gradually become the symbol of the local cuisine. There is also chicken with nigella seeds, couscous with sumach, and *mezgueldi*, a tagine of lamb with caramelized onions. Add to the delights of the palate vestiges from the past. Visit the Koutoubia mosque, the beacon of Almohad art, the famed square Jemaà el Fna, the koranic school Medersa Ben Youssef, the gardens of Menara, and the old medina.

Fes, founded by Moulay Idriss, was the refuge for Muslims and Jews who were forced out of Andalousia beginning in the ninth century. The last refugees arrived in the labyrinthine city in AD 1492, as the final tears fell on the cheeks of the last sultan of Grenada, Boabdil, who was defeated by the Catholic kings.

Fes el Jedid, a living mélange of cultures, was declared capital of the empire in AD 1250. In the dazzling homes that conceal their beauty behind the high walls of the old city of Fes, refined dishes are presented with style and grace. The cuisine of Fes resembles that of Tlemcen, a shared heritage from Andalousia of which both cities are proud. Fes has its lamb and squash tagine with honey; its vermicelli couscous with pigeons; its various recipes for carrots, savory, sweet or with cumin; its pigeon pastilla; and its partridge couscous. A must-see is the Karaouiyine mosque, the most prestigious Arab Muslim university of the medieval world, built to the glory of Allah in the ninth century, where precious manuscripts from the libraries of Grenada, Seville, and Cordoba found refuge after Spain fell to the Reconquista. Don't miss the Danan synagogue, built in the seventeenth century in the *mellah*, the Jewish quarter, or the marvelous *souk* (market).

Meknes, the former capital of Moulay Ismaël, the Alawite sovereign, is the least well-known of the four imperial cities as a tourist destination. Modest in size, Meknes has retained the languor that is customary in provincial cities. In a city with a large Jewish population, tolerance reigns. And the cuisine is a conscious reflection of this openness. If it is true that the Jewish community has its own recipes, like chicken pâté, potato pastilla or stuffed

Tanjia marrakshia is a dish made by men for men. This meat dish takes the name of the *tanjia*, or earthenware amphora, in which it is cooked. Sealed with paper and string, the amphora is baked for as long as four hours.

mutton intestine, Muslims were also proud of their own cuisine that was similar to that of nearby Fes. But inhabitants of Meknes are supposedly stingy with their wealth and it is no accident that one of their specialties is called "the hen has flown." Guests are promised a dish of chicken and garbanzo beans but what a surprise to see plates served only with beans! When the host is asked where the meat is, he invariably replies that the hen has flown off.

Rabat, the modern capital, has attracted many guests to its table. If the bazaars are not as showy as those of Fes or Marrakech, it is because the city prefers calm and modernity. Here reigns the cuisine of the *makhzen*, the official cuisine that has ties to every region of Morocco and the neighboring countries. Home cooking, rich and varied, is in every way astonishing. Some recipes are carefully guarded secrets like the famous *bal farkh* couscous made with sea bass.

A coastal city, Rabat shares the secrets of the sea with the other coastal towns of Assafi and Essaouira, but Rabat has no equal when it comes to cooking shad, a fish similar to the sardine. Assafi and Essaouira are famous for serving *baddaz*, couscous made from sweet corn, garnished with conger eel heads, and fried moray eel with honey.

In Rabat, you will also find *kaak*, a delicious cake, or *zemata*, a dish made with seeds (in Oujda, the town on the Algerian border, it is made with young wheat and covered with figs.)

Although the city of Tetouan is not strictly speaking an imperial city, its history renders it indispensable. In its vast memory reside the splendors of Muslim Andalousia, its riches, and its subtle perfumes. A direct heir to the culinary traditions of Grenada, Tetouan is also one of the only Moroccan cities to have been subjected to the influence of the Ottomans as the presence of bakhlava and *ktaifs* (a pastry made with shredded filo) attests, giving a special accent to border and coastal towns. *Pastilla* of chicken with preserved lemons also hails from this area.

BELOW: A fountain in an old residence in Fes.
NEXT PAGE: Riads are elegant homes discreetly nestled in the heart of medinas, which house a central patio decorated with a fountain.

Food and Religion
Abstinence and culinary feats in honor of Islam

An active member of the Islamic community, or *umma*, Morocco proudly proclaims its religious heritage. The king, in addition to his role as chief executive, is also the spiritual guide for his subjects. The Alowite dynasty, from which both the King of Morocco and the King of Jordan are descended, is one of the branches that traces its roots directly back to the prophet Mohammed. Religion is very present in the hearts of all Moroccans.

In the words of a nineteenth century French traveler, Eugène Fromentin, as taken from his journal published in AD 1857 as *A Summer in the Sahara,* to understand that food and the divine form a whole in Morocco, "you must see that in Arab beliefs eating and giving something to eat are solemn acts and that a *diffa* (feast) is a great lesson in savoir vivre, generosity, and sharing attentions. Take note that it is not due to any social obligations…but in virtue of a divine inspiration…and, to use their words, it is as a messenger from God that the traveler is welcomed by his host. Their politeness therefore is explained not by conventions but rather is based on religious principle. They practice it with the same respect they have for all things that are holy and do so as an act of devotion. Therefore it is not at all a laughing matter to see robust men, in warrior's attire with their amulets round their necks, stoically performing the small household duties that in Europe fall to women; seeing their large hands, hardened by the handling of horses and the practice of arms, serving at the table, slicing meat before serving it to you, showing the best cut in the back of a mutton, holding the carafe or, between each course, offering serviettes made of handwoven wool. These attentions, which in our world appear puerile, perhaps even ridiculous, here become touching because of the contrast that exists between the man and the humble tasks he performs with strength and dignity.

Celebrations such as family visits, weddings, and circumcisions are all occasions for the lady of the house to show off her culinary talents. Likewise, for religious holidays such as the Prophet's birthday, Laylat al Qadr, Laylat al Seghir, Ashoura, and the month of Ramadan, daily fares give way to festive and culinary celebrations. Among the Five Pillars of Islam, Ramadan holds a special place. The

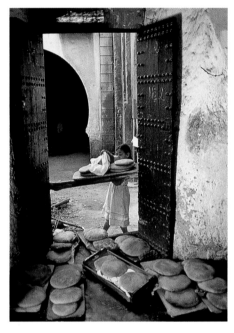

Prophet wanted this to test the faith of the converts, and fasting lasts 30 days. It is a way of bringing families together to share the food that will deliver the soul at sunset.

Unlike Christian fasting which is considered penitence, atonement for sins, and a battle against natural instincts, fasting during Ramadan is for a Muslim a way to serve God, to pay homage to Him. Thus Ramadan has become a period of joy, and pride for the believer who is given the opportunity to manifest his belonging to Islam. It is a period of celebration that is given concrete expression around the table in the form of delicious foods.

From the time Muslims get up, they must avoid any transgression; not the merest drop of coffee must taint their empty cup. And because nothing is as present as what is absent, mothers outdo themselves during the sacred month to produce all their culinary dreams both savory, and especially sweet. Everything is timed and planned. People are purified and pray, they pardon, they enter the kitchen more often than usual in an effort to trick their hunger. It is a wonderful month, where days extend into the languorous night. Muslims live at night and sleep in the morning. Women create, invent, or reproduce old recipes. Men, unable to go to the café, fill the streets, the mosques, and the markets, which become more colorful than usual. At night, there is a ballet of dishes and sweets, but the queen of the month is *harira*. Dates too are served. Is it not said that the Prophet himself broke his fast with dates and milk? Round tables, tablecloths, earthenware and porcelain bowls, glasses of milk, dates, *shebakiya*…he who has not visited a Moroccan house at this time has seen nothing, smelled nothing. Never are so many scents, colors, and desires brought together as they are for Ramadan.

After breaking the fast each evening, contented believers throng the alleyways. Nothing is better than a full stomach. Then comes *iisha*, the dinner hour and time for the last prayer, and for a second time we go back to the table: meat and poultry, asparagus with eggs, fruits, salads, and of course sweets of all kinds: *grioush, zalabiya, halwat tourk* (Turkish halva), gazelle horns from Fes, and *makrout* from Tlemcen.

Then comes the twenty-seventh day. The day of days

that announces the Night of Destiny (or Night of Power) during which anything can happen. It is said that the Prophet Mohammed received his first revelation in the last ten days of the month of Ramadan, and the *ulamas* (religious leaders) decided to end the event on the twenty-seventh day of the month. Since that time, a lamb has been sacrificed by the richest families, a chicken by the less well-to-do, and couscous is prepared for the mosque where it will be distributed to the least fortunate. In the last few years, it would seem that due to a resurgence of faith, prayers last until dawn. Then comes Laylet al Seghir. All the children wear new clothes. Everywhere houses are filled with cakes made during the last week of Ramadan. Neighbors and cousins meet to blanch and skin almonds or to steam dates. Dozens and dozens of eggs are broken, sesame seeds toasted, anise seeds ground. Everybody participates to give the festivities a special air.

Each family rivals the next with inventions. One will ask a cousin from Algeria or another from a different region of Morocco for a recipe unknown in these parts. On the morning of Laylet al Seghir, all the aromas regain their rightful place after a month of absence: the boiling coffee flows once again in the glasses and white cups.

Among the other principles of the Koran, there are restrictions that everyone must obey. Pork is deemed to be illicit, as is any animal that has not been bled. An animal is not slaughtered, it is sacrificed. Blood renders flesh impure. If an animal has not been bled in accordance with religious law, then it is carrion (*djifa*) and banned.

This rule also applies to game. All wild animals that are not specifically banned by the Holy Book may be eaten. When one wants to kill animals whose flesh can be eaten, one must turn to face the East and cut its throat while saying "*Allahu Akbar!*" (God is great). Where animals that live in water are concerned, the doctrines differ, depending on the various rites. Some allow the eating of all such animals, but others have exceptions—frogs, in particular, are the subject of much debate. On the other hand, cricket flesh is legal, as long as it is captured alive and killed by a Muslim. It is said that the Prophet's wives considered it to be a delicacy. The most sacred food in Morocco is bread. Given by God, it is the food most surrounded by tradition. If a Muslim Moroccan finds a piece of bread on the ground, tradition dictates that he pick it up, kiss it, and place it somewhere where it will not be soiled.

OPPOSITE: In large cities, every neighborhood has one or more public bread ovens where you can leave your bread, and even your cakes or *mechoui* (barbecued lamb), to be cooked.
ABOVE: Street food is a Moroccan tradition. There are the classic dishes and there are the masters who prepare them. Here is a *mechoui* (barbecued lamb) "specialist" from Marrakech.

Moroccan Hospitality

Whether very poor or incredibly rich, Moroccans all share a truly exceptional sense of hospitality. It is not unusual to see that a friend of the family is often better looked after than the family's own son. The guest, treated with respect and honored with an engaging smile, must never under any circumstances refuse what he is offered or he risks bringing shame on his hosts. Hospitality is so sacred that members of the family will bend over backwards to accommodate a visiting friend.

It must be said that in Morocco, as in most Arab and Muslim countries, the whole family comes together for meals, men in one room, women in another, though this practice is quickly losing ground in the urban centers of Casablanca and Rabat. At mealtimes, each diner takes his or her place around a low table upon which the couscous or the tagine is served from a common dish, and nimbly uses thumb, index, and middle fingers of the right hand to serve himself a piece of meat or a little semolina.

The symbolism associated with bread is very strong. If someone tries to share a piece of bread that has been given him with another guest at the table, it may be thought that he is looking for a fight with the person who originally served the bread to him.

Traditional clay tagine pots are slowly disappearing from the Moroccan table in response to changing tastes. Today it is not surprising to see a Chinese serving dish on an embroidered Berber tablecloth. The tea ceremony remains a special moment when entertaining guests. Even though it is a relatively recent practice—it was probably introduced in the eighteenth or nineteenth centuries—tea is particularly valued and has quickly become one of the most powerful

symbols of the Moroccan kingdom.

"The whole universe is found in a teapot," writes Abdallah Zrika. "Or more accurately, the *sinia* (circular platter) represents the earth, the teapot the heavens, and the glasses rain; the heavens by way of the rain is joined to the earth."

At first reserved only for the very wealthy because of its exorbitant cost, the consumption of tea quickly became widespread. In the palaces of Marrakech, on the slopes of the Atlas Mountains or in the blazing heat of a nomad's tent, the infusion remains the drink favored by all Moroccans. Tea invariably concludes a meal and figures in discussions at any sidewalk café. It is served at breakfast, during the morning break, after lunch, as an apéritif, and after dinner. It is present at every hour of a Moroccan's day.

Preparing and serving the drink is a true art. A layer of tea is placed in glimmering teapots, followed by fresh mint leaves, broken lumps of sugar, and boiling water. Sometimes absinthe leaves are added to give the tea a slightly bitter edge. The host takes the teapot and pours the precious drink into a small glass from as high as he can. The contents are then poured back into the teapot and the pouring repeated until the mint, tea, and sugar are perfectly combined. Only then does the satisfied host hand each guest a steaming glass of tea.

All Roads Lead to the Souk

A festival of colors and scents

Every Moroccan city harbors a medina, the old quarter where the past still echoes clearly and the flow of passers-by is never-ending. Here are found the craftsmen, the traders, and the gossip that will be the subject of lively discussions in the *hammam*, or traditional steam baths.

A treasure trove worthy of Ali Baba, and guarded by massive gates, the *souk* is a succession of narrow, often covered, alleyways with back-to-back shops that are barely bigger than a linen cupboard. Tinsmiths, grocers, butchers, pastry chefs, tailors, spice merchants, and cake vendors meet daily and co-exist in indescribable mayhem.

If Moroccan cuisine enjoys such prestige, it is because it has, over the centuries, learned to refine its judgment and satisfy the demands of the palate, the eyes, and the nose as few cuisines have. Arab doctors used spices very early on in their remedies. They also knew how to give their patients a taste for finer things. Spices play an important role in their remedies, and are used in preparing the most astonishing recipes. In a society in which restrictions abound, there exists a whole range of local remedies that have a powerful following—from love potions to cures for sterility, spices hold the answer to all our everyday woes. Grandmothers' recipes live long in Morocco. In the home, women often deploy their imagination, ingenuity, and skill to stay in good health. Swallowing two spoonfuls of cumin to counter stomach flu requires a little bravery, but these little tricks heal the body and ease the mind.

Morocco is the birth place of the rare and surprising *ras el hanout*, "head of the shop" in Arabic, the heady mixture of twenty-seven spices, the secret of which is jealously guarded in the memories of a handful of shopkeepers in the dark alleys of the *souks* in Fes and Marrakech.

In the *souk*, the merchant, perched atop his colorful displays, calls to the passer-by. Drunken on the spell of words and smells, transfixed by the shimmering colors, the shopper purchases caraway seeds, cloves, nigella seeds, cinnamon, mace, and cumin in little folded bags. Once home, the man hands his wife the precious sachets with which she will prepare the dishes for the next meal.

Odors, flavors, and scents play an important role in Morocco. They are synonymous with gates that lead to the sublime. In every home, hidden in small containers or old battered tins, are the spices that give Moroccan cuisine a touch of color and exude their delicate perfume.

In the *souk*, different activities are located in different quarters: the *baboush* (Moroccan slippers) *souk*, the henna *souk*, the *souk* of the luthiers, the copperware *souk*, and the vegetable market.

Cooking in Morocco

A variety of traditional and modern cooking utensils are found in Moroccan kitchens today

One of the most important kitchen utensils is the *tagine*. The term tagine describes both the food—a long-cooked stew, usually of lamb or chicken—and the earthenware vessel in which it is cooked. A tagine has a round, shallow base and a tall, pointed cover and tagines are prepared by long simmering over an open fire or a bed of charcoal. A heat diffuser, a metal plate with a wooden handle, is essential for cooking a tagine over an electric element or gas flame. The metal plate stops the base of the tagine from burning and spreads the heat for more even cooking.

Traditionally, a terracotta *majmar*, or charcoal brazier, was often used by families in Northern Morocco to both provide heat in the winter and to heat tagines. Typically the *majmar* was taken to the local baker to fill with the hot coals that had been used to cook the bread.

A *tanjia* describes both the food and the earthenware amphora that is used to cook the specialty of Marrakech, *tanjia marrakshia*. The amphora containing the meat and spices is simply sealed with paper and string and baked for several hours.

Couscous, the staple food of Morocco, resembles tiny balls of dough which are steamed and served like rice, often mixed with a tagine stew. The balls of dough are made not by kneading but by sprinkling salted water into a *gasaa*—a large dish once made of clay or wood but today mostly available in stainless steel or aluminum—containing flour (from wheat, barley, or maize) while the fingers of the right hand are slowly raked through the flour causing the dough to form tiny balls which are then dried. (A *gasaa* is also used to knead dough for bread.) Couscous is steamed in a *quadra wa alkaskas*, or couscoussier, which has two parts: the lower part for cooking the vegetables and the meat or fish, and the top—which has a perforated bottom—for steaming the couscous.

Ghorbal

The teapot or *l'barrade* is the symbol of Moroccan hospitality. It is made from hand-hammered tin, silver plate, or stainless steel and has a long spout for the pour which is especially important. Tea is also served in glasses, rather than in cups. Many Moroccans have unique collections of these colorful little glasses, embellished with different designs.

A large circular tray, or *sinia*, is traditionally used to serve tea and other treats to guests (page 25). These trays are often silver or brass and elaborately engraved.

Teapot

Other traditional kitchen utensils that are still seen today include the *ghorbal*, a sieve made from pierced leather that is used to make *smen*, and the *chtato*, or silk-lined sieve. Cooking pots and pans include the *maqla*, or copper skillet, the *quarda* and *tanjir*, different kinds of large copper stewing pots, and the *tanjra* which was originally a clay pot although today, the stainless steel version is more widely used. A large round, lined copper pan, called a *tbsil dyal bastela*, is used to bake the popular flaky pies called *b'stilla*, although a greased baking dish is often used.

Steamer

Authentic Moroccan Ingredients

Almonds are cultivated in Morocco and along with other nuts play an important role in both sweet and savory dishes. Almonds are usually blanched and peeled and sometimes ground into a paste for pastry fillings. Fresh, unroasted almonds are available in bulk and in packages in most supermarkets. Store them in the refrigerator to extend their shelf life.

Aniseed—the Arabic name for this spice means "that which does good." Aniseed are sweet, aromatic seeds with licorice flavor. They are used both whole and ground in pastries and in some main dishes like Chicken with Anise. Aniseed is available in most supermarkets.

Caraway seeds are similar to cumin seeds in appearance. They have a pungent aroma and a sweet, tangy flavor. Caraway seeds are most often used in salads, and especially in *harira*, the famed Moroccan soup (see page 46). They are available in the spice section of most supermarkets. You can substitute aniseed or fennel seeds, but the flavor will be slightly different.

Coriander leaves, or cilantro, is a leafy green annual herb. The fresh leaves are often used together with flat-leaf (Italian) parsley to season fish and poultry. Coriander leaves are available fresh in most supermarkets.

Cumin is the dried seed of an herb that belongs to the parsley family. Its nutty, peppery flavor adds interest to carrots, fava beans and *kefta* (ground meat). Ground cumin should be used sparingly because it can easily overpower a dish. Cumin is available in the spice section of most supermarkets.

Fava beans or broad beans are large, flat beans that range in color from yellow to green to tan. They are used fresh, frozen and dried and often appear in salads and soups, where their nutty flavor is appreciated. Fava beans have a tough skin that should be removed by blanching them before cooking. Substitute lima beans.

Fenugreek is the dry yellow seed of the aromatic plant of the same name. It is most commonly used in spice mixtures but is also used to season breads. Fenugreek has a very intense flavor that is similar to curry. Use it sparingly—too much can make a dish unbearably bitter. Fenugreek is available in Indian groceries and health food stores. Omit if unavailable.

Flat-leaf parsley, also known as Italian parsley, is used in almost all Moroccan dishes. It is indispensable for the preparation of *shermoula*, a mixture of herbs and spices. Flat-leaf parsley is easily grown at home. It is available at most supermarkets.

Ginger is often used in dry powdered form in Morocco. It is considered to be an aphrodisiac. Use it sparingly— its sweet, spicy flavor can overpower a dish. Ground ginger is available in the spice section of most supermarkets.

Harissa is a hot, red paste made with chili peppers, herbs and spices and is popular in Morocco and North Africa. It is often made at home by blending red chilies with caraway, coriander, salt, and oil but it is also available in cans or tubes at North African and Arab groceries. To make a suitable substitute, combine two finely chopped fresh red chilies with ½ teaspoon each of ground cumin and ground coriander.

Jben is a soft cheese made in Morocco from cow's milk or raw goat's milk. It has a fresh mild taste and is sometimes brined to impart a salty flavor. Substitute a mild variety of goat cheese.

Mint is the defining herbal flavor in Morocco. It is unthinkable to end a meal without mint tea. Fresh mint is available in most supermarkets.

Nigella seeds (also called black onion seeds), have a pungent oregano-like flavor. They are often found on bread, but also appear in some prepared dishes like Nigella Seed Chicken. Nigella seeds can be found in Indian or Middle Eastern groceries and health food stores. Substitute black caraway seeds.

Two types of olives are typically found on the Moroccan table. Oil or salt-cured black olives that have a very strong, bitter flavor—these are best used in cooking and not for snacking. Green, red or purple marinated olives are eaten on their own and are also added to tagines. You can buy Moroccan olives in gourmet shops or Arab groceries. You can substitute Kalamata olives where black olives are called for.

Orange flower water is a fragrant, distilled of bitter orange oil that is used to flavor both savory and sweet dishes. A little goes a long way so be sure to add only a few drops at a time. You can purchase it in gourmet shops or Middle Eastern specialty shops. Alternatively, grate an orange and soak the grated rind in sweet white wine for 24 hours. Strain and use in place of orange flower water.

Paprika is a dried ground seasoning made from red bell pepper. There are several varieties of paprika—hot and smoked are the most popular ones. Paprika is used to add both color and flavor to dishes. The sweet variety is available in most supermarkets.

Pigeon meat is dark, flavorful and very tender. Gourmet markets and Asian markets sell it but it can be quite expensive. You can substitute chicken, Cornish game hens or quail.

Pine nuts are small ivory-colored seeds collected from the pine cones of stone pine trees. When raw, the seeds have a soft texture and a sweet, buttery flavor. They are often lightly toasted to bring out their flavor and to add a crunchy texture. Pine nuts are harvested by hand and are therefore expensive. They can be found in most supermarkets.

Preserved lemons are made from Meyer lemons that have been pickled in their own juices and salt. They are available bottled in gourmet shops or you can make your own using the recipe given on page 35.

Quinces are pear-shaped fruits with a sour, astringent flavor and a perfume-like fragrance. Used mostly for jam and jelly, they develop a pink color when cooked. Meat and fruit are frequently cooked together in Moroccan dishes and quinces are often added to lamb stews. If you can't find fresh quinces, substitute Granny Smith or another tart variety of apple.

Ras el hanout or "top of the shop," is a finely balanced composition of twenty-seven spices. It has a floral fragrance and a robust, curry-like flavor. It lends a beautiful golden color to simmered dishes. *Ras el hanout* is available in Middle Eastern or Arabic specialty shops or you can make your own with the following recipe.

Ras el Hanout

1 teaspoon ground cumin
1 teaspoon ground ginger
1 teaspoon ground turmeric
1 teaspoon salt
$3/4$ teaspoon ground cinnamon
$3/4$ teaspoon ground black pepper
$1/2$ teaspoon ground white pepper
$1/2$ teaspoon ground coriander
$1/2$ teaspoon cayenne pepper
$1/2$ teaspoon ground allspice
$1/2$ teaspoon ground nutmeg
$1/4$ teaspoon ground cloves

Combine all the spices in a bowl and mix well. Stored in an airtight container, the spice blend keep for 1 month.

Rosewater adds a distinctive flavor to Moroccan sweets. It is made by steaming dried rose petals and distilling the liquid. You can find rosewater in gourmet shops and Middle Eastern specialty stores.

Saffon is originally from India and is known as the queen of spices. It is picked with near religious fervor before dawn, which explains its price. Be careful not to buy counterfeits which are sometimes made with silk from corn husks and a little oil. Saffron is always used in festive dishes. You can substitute ground turmeric though it has neither the subtlety nor the strength.

Semolina is a flour made from coarsely ground durum wheat and is the basic ingredient for making couscous. When cooked, it has a nutty flavor and a chewy texture that serves as a foundation for other Moroccan dishes much the same way as rice does in Asia. Semolina flour is available in specialty shops and some well-stocked supermarkets.

Sesame seeds are used both ground and whole and are often toasted to bring out their nutty flavor. They are used on breads, in pastries and as a garnish. Sesame seeds can be purchased in bulk or packaged in most supermarkets. Since they have a high oil content, store them in an airtight container in the refrigerator to prevent them from becoming rancid.

Smen is a traditional cooking oil with a pungent and distinct flavor. It is made from butter that is cooked at a high temperature, salted and then strained. The liquid is then aged in an earthenware container. Substitute ghee or salted butter. Alternatively, make your own *smen* with the recipe for Clarified Butter given on page 34.

Thyme is fragrant herb that grows abundantly in the wild in Morocco. It has a faint lemony flavor and powerful antiseptic and preservative qualities. Because fresh thyme has a mild flavor it is difficult to overpower a dish. Use the small, tender leaves and discard the woody stems. Use fresh thyme rather than dried thyme whenever possible.

Turmeric is a rhizome with an earthy, bitter flavor. The dried ground root is probably best known as an ingredient in curry powder, but it is also widely used as a coloring agent—it naturally lends simmered dishes a rich golden color. Ground turmeric is available in the spice section of most supermarkets.

Warka Pastry Leaf is a very fine pastry used to make *B'stilla,* the well-known Moroccan pie. It is also used to make a variety of other pastries. With a bit of effort, you can make your own *warka* pastry leaf using the recipe on page 35 but fresh or frozen filo pastry sheets that you purchase in the supermarket also make a good substitute.

Basic Recipes

Preparing Couscous

Couscous is the name given to both the uncooked semolina grains and the cooked dish. A staple food of much of North Africa, couscous is now very popular in Europe and North America. Many brands of couscous are marked "instant" and offer instructions for cooking in a microwave oven. If you want a more authentic couscous, I encourage you to try the traditional Moroccan way which is easily mastered and takes about 45 minutes to prepare:

1 Wet 3 cups (500 g) of dried couscous with a little water in a large shallow bowl or casserole dish. Rake your fingers through the grains so that they are evenly moistened. Line a steamer basket or couscoussier with a cheesecloth and bring the water in the pot under the steamer basket to a simmer. Cover and steam for 30 minutes.

2 Pour the couscous, now a compact mass, back into the large dish that you used to moisten it. Using a fork, break up the "cake" that has formed, adding a little cold water to help break up any lumps. Add salt to taste and return the couscous to the steamer basket.

3 Steam for a few more minutes. Once the steam rises through the grains, pour the couscous into the dish one last time. Add 2 tablespoons of butter and mix it into the couscous to separate the grains. Serve hot.

Step 1: Moisten the couscous with a little water in a large shallow dish.

Step 2: Break up the steamed couscous and add a little cold water.

Step 3: Return the couscous to the steamer for the last stage of cooking.

Clarified Butter   Smen

Making *smen*, or salted clarified butter, is a Berber tradition. The butter is first clarified—it is melted and the solids are removed—then it is sometimes simmered with herbs, strained, and salted. In Morocco, *smen* is often buried and aged until it becomes very pungent. Salted butter and ghee are suitable substitutes.

1 cup (250 g) salted butter

Cooking time: 25 mins

1 Melt the butter in a heavy saucepan over low heat and simmer gently for-for 25 minutes or until the milk solids are golden. Strain through a fine sieve into a glass jar and store in the refrigerator.

Warka Pastry Leaf

The technique used in this recipe requires a lot of patience and dexterity. Filo pastry is a very good substitute and is well worth the time and effort saved.

4 cups (600 g) flour
Pinch of salt
1 tablespoon olive oil
2 cups (500 ml) lukewarm water

Makes approximately 10 sheets
Preparation time: 1 hour + 1 hour
  for dough to rest

1 Mix the flour, salt, and oil together in a bowl. Gradually add the water, kneading into a soft, elastic dough. Sprinkle with a little more water, cover and set aside to rest for 1 hour.
2 Set a skillet (preferably copper) on top of a pot of water, with the underside facing up. Bring the water to a simmer over medium heat and grease the upturned skillet. When the metal is hot, reduce the heat to low. Take a handful of dough and quickly touch the lump of dough to the skillet. It will leave a thin round film on the pan. Repeat several times, leaving no gaps between each film, forming a large, almost transparent sheet.
3 Remove the sheet carefully and keep under a damp cloth until ready to use. Repeat with the remaining dough, greasing the upturned skillet before making a new pastry sheet.

Folding Briwattes Pastries

Briwattes (pages 40–41) are pastries made with Warka Pastry Leaf (or store-bought filo pastry) with nut, rice or savory fillings. They are fried in hot oil until golden brown. The photos below illustrate how the pastries are folded.

Step 1: Cut the sheets of pastry into strips and place a teaspoon of filling at one end.

Step 2: Fold the corner of the pastry over at a right angle to form a triangle.

Step 3: Continue to fold the triangle at right angles. The last fold should be tucked in to seal the pastry.

Preserved Lemons

8–10 ripe lemons
$^1/_2$ cup (125 g) kosher or sea salt

Preparation Time: 10 mins + 1 month
  to marinate and preserve

1 Clean the lemons thoroughly with a brush under running water. Slice each lemon into quarters without cutting it all the way through to the base. Rub each lemon with a generous amount of salt.
2 Pack the lemons into a large, sterilized jar, sprinkling additional salt between each layer. If necessary, add the juice from 1 lemon and boiling water to cover before sealing the jar. Store in a cool, dark place for 1 month.
3 Be sure to rinse a preserved lemon before using it in a recipe. The pulp is quite bitter—you may want to remove it and use only the rind. Store the opened jar in the refrigerator.

Authentic Moroccan Recipes

City Bread

City bread is usually made with only white flour. For a different presentation, brush the loaves with beaten egg yolk and sprinkle with kosher or sea salt, aniseed and/or sesame seeds before baking.

3 teaspoons active dried yeast
2 cups (500 ml) warm water
4$^1/_2$ cups (675 g) flour
$^1/_2$ teaspoon salt
1 tablespoon vegetable oil
2 tablespoons cornmeal

1 Dissolve the yeast in a small amount of the warm water and set it aside.
2 Sift the flour into a large bowl, form a well in the center and add the salt and the dissolved yeast. Mix and add the warm water while kneading vigorously. The dough should be soft and elastic. Add a little more warm water, if necessary.
3 Divide the dough into two equal parts. Roll each into a ball and lightly oil the surface of each with vegetable oil. Flatten each ball into a disk, place on a clean kitchen towel and set aside to rise in a warm place for 1 hour.
4 Heat the oven to 400°F (200°C). Press the dough with your finger. If it returns to its original shape, it is ready. If you leave a fingerprint, let it rise another 15 minutes.
5 Sprinkle a baking sheet with the cornmeal. Slide the loaves onto the sheet and into the oven and bake until golden, approximately 25 minutes.

Preparation Time: 1 hour + 1 hour to rise
Baking Time: 25 mins

Country Bread

Country bread is made with both white and whole wheat flour and has a coarse crumb that is suitable for soaking up sauces.

3 teaspoons active dried yeast
2 cups (500 ml) warm water
3 cups (450 g) flour
1$^1/_2$ cups (225 g) whole wheat flour
1 teaspoon salt
1 tablespoon vegetable oil
Pinch of kosher salt
3 tablespoons cornmeal

1 Dissolve the yeast in a little of the warm water and set it aside.
2 Combine the flours in a large bowl. Make a well in the center and add 1 teaspoon of salt and the dissolved yeast.
3 Gradually add the remaining warm water while kneading the dough vigorously. The dough should be soft. If it is too stiff, add a little more warm water.
4 Divide the dough into two equal parts. Roll each into a ball and lightly coat the surface of each with vegetable oil. Flatten each into a disk and sprinkle the tops with kosher salt and cornmeal. Place on a clean kitchen towel and set aside to rise in a warm place for 1 hour.
5 Preheat the oven to 400°F (200°C). Sprinkle a baking sheet with cornmeal and lift the rounds onto the sheet. Bake in the oven until golden, abpproximately 25 minutes.

Preparation Time: 1 hour + 1 hour to rise
Baking Time: 25 mins

LEFT: Country Bread (on top), City Bread with sesame seeds (in middle), and City Bread (on bottom).

Eggplant Salad

2 lbs (1 kg) globe eggplants, stems discarded, sliced lengthwise into 4 to 6 pieces
1 bunch flat-leaf parsley, stems discarded, leaves finely chopped
Large pinch of salt
2 tablespoons vinegar
3 tablespoons olive oil
1 teaspoon paprika
Pinch of ground cumin
3 cloves garlic, peeled and crushed

1 Blanch the eggplants for 10 minutes in salted boiling water, drain and set aside.
2 Combine the parsley, salt, vinegar, oil, spices, and garlic in a large bowl. to make a dressing. Dip each piece of cooked eggplant in this dressing and arrange on a serving platter. Serve hot or cold.

Preparation Time: 20 mins
Cooking Time: 10 mins

Fresh Fava Bean Salad

1 lb (500 g) fresh fava beans in the pod, shelled to yield
$1/2$ lb (250 g) shelled beans
4 cups (1 liter) water
1 tablespoon olive oil
$1/2$ teaspoon ground cumin
2 small cloves garlic, peeled and crushed
$1/2$ teaspoon salt
Crushed red pepper, to taste

1 Wash the beans and remove the germ but don't peel them. Blanch for 5 to 8 minutes in salted water. Drain and place in a salad bowl.
2 Combine the olive oil, cumin, garlic, salt, and chili in a small bowl then pour over the beans and mix thoroughly. Serve hot with another drizzle of olive oil.

Preparation Time: 20 mins
Cooking Time: 10 mins

Zucchini Sautéed with Cumin and Paprika

1 lb (500 g) zucchini, stems removed, halved lengthwise, then quartered
$1^1/2$ tablespoons olive oil
2 cloves garlic, peeled and crushed
$1/2$ bunch flat-leaf parsley, chopped
$1/2$ teaspoon salt
$1/2$ teaspoon ground cumin
$1/2$ teaspoon paprika
2 tablespoons fresh lemon juice

1 Blanch the zucchini in salted boiling water for 5–8 minutes. Drain and set aside.
2 Heat the olive oil in a pan and sauté the garlic, parsley, salt, cumin, and paprika. Cook for 3–5 minutes, stirring. Add the zucchini and stir gently for another 5–7 minutes. Add the lemon juice. Serve hot or cold.

Preparation Time: 15 mins
Cooking Time: 20 mins

Carrot and Walnut Salad

3 large carrots, peeled and grated
Juice of 1 orange
1 teaspoon sugar
$1/2$ teaspoon ground cinnamon
1 teaspoon orange flower water
$1/4$ cup (125 g) shelled walnuts

1 Combine the grated carrot, orange juice, sugar, cinnamon, and orange flower water in a large bowl. Mix well and chill. Serve garnished with the walnuts.

Preparation Time: 20 mins + time to chill

Tomato Jam

This jam is delicious on bread or on plain couscous.

$1/4$ cup (60 g) butter
12 medium-sized ripe tomatoes, peeled, deseeded and diced
1 teaspoon salt
1 teaspoon ground cinnamon
Pinch of ground nutmeg
1 tablespoon rosewater
$1/2$ cup (125 ml) honey
$1/3$ cup (50 g) sesame seeds

1 Melt the butter in a pot over medium heat. Add the tomatoes, salt, spices, and rosewater. Mix well and cook for 5 minutes. Reduce the heat and simmer for 40 minutes or until most of the liquid has evaporated, stirring occasionally.
2 Add the honey, mix well and cook for another 15 minutes.
3 Store in a sterilized jar in the refrigerator for up to 1 week.

Preparation Time: 5 mins
Cooking Time: 1 hour

Carrots Sautéed with Cumin

This salad can be served hot or cold.

3 large carrots, peeled, halved and
  then quartered lengthwise
2 tablespoons olive oil
2 cloves garlic, peeled and crushed
1/2 bunch flat-leaf parsley, chopped
1/2 teaspoon ground black pepper
1/2 teaspoon ground cumin
Juice of 1/2 lemon
Black olives for garnish

1 Blanch the carrots in salted boiling water for 8 to 10 minutes. Drain.
2 Heat the oil in a pan and sauté the carrots, garlic, parsley, pepper, and cumin. Add the lemon juice and serve garnished with olives.

Preparation Time: 5 mins
Cooking Time: 15 mins

Roasted Spiced Eggplant Purée

2 lbs (1 kg) globe eggplants
5 tablespoons olive oil
2 cloves garlic, peeled and crushed
1 bunch parsley, leaves chopped
1 bunch fresh coriander leaves
  (cilantro), chopped
2 medium-sized tomatoes, peeled,
  deseeded, and cubed
1/2 teaspoon ground cumin
1/2 teaspoon paprika
1/2 teaspoon ground black pepper
1 teaspoon salt
1 lemon, one half juiced, the other cut
  into wedges
12 black olives

1 Preheat oven to 500°F (250°C). Split the skin of the eggplants lengthwise to prevent them from bursting while cooking. Place them on a baking sheet and bake for 40 minutes, turning occasionally. Once cool, remove the stems and skin. Cut the flesh into cubes and crush with a fork.
2 Heat the oil in pan and sauté the eggplant, garlic, chopped herbs, tomatoes, spices, salt, and lemon juice. Cook for 30 minutes. Serve hot or cold garnished with the lemon wedges and black olives.

Preparation Time: 20 mins
Cooking Time: 1 hour + 15 mins

Roasted Bell Peppers

2 green bell peppers
2 red bell peppers
1 tomato, peeled, deseeded, and cubed
1 clove garlic, minced freshly ground
Pinch each of salt and pepper
Pinch of ground cumin
4 tablespoons olive oil

1 Grill or broil the bell peppers in the oven, approximately 30 minutes, turning regularly, until the skins are completely blistered. Place in a sealed plastic bag or wrap in aluminum foil. When cool enough to handle, peel, deseed, and rinse the peppers in warm water then pat dry.
2 Slice the peppers into thin strips and arrange on a plate. Add the cubed tomato and sprinkle with the minced garlic. Season with salt, pepper, and a pinch of cumin. Drizzle with olive oil, then toss and serve warm or cold.

Preparation Time: 45 mins
Cooking Time: 30 min

Rice Pastries
Briwattes b' Arroz

2 cups (500 ml) water
2 cups (500 ml) low-fat milk
Pinch of salt
1 tablespoon sugar
$^3/_4$ cup (150 g) short-grain rice, rinsed
$^1/_2$ cup (125 g) butter
1 tablespoon orange flower water
2 teaspoons cinnamon
6 sheets filo pastry or Warka Pastry
  Leaf (page 35)
Oil for deep-frying
$^3/_8$ cup (100 g) almonds, fried in oil
  6–8 minutes then roughly chopped

1 Bring the water and milk to a boil in a saucepan. Add the rice, salt and sugar, and simmer, uncovered, for 10 minutes. Add the butter and continue to cook for another 10 minutes. Remove from the heat when the rice is tender, add the orange flower water, cinnamon and the chopped almonds and set aside to cool.
2 Cut each sheet of filo into 4 strips, place 1 teaspoon of cooked, cooled rice at one end, fold down the corner to form a triangle and continue folding at right angles, then tuck the end into the last fold to seal (page 35). Repeat until all the filo has been used up.
3 In a large pan, heat the oil over medium heat. Fry the rice triangles until they are golden, about 5 minutes, then remove with a slotted spoon and drain on paper towels. Arrange the triangles on a plate and sprinkle with cinnamon.

Preparation Time: 1 hour
Cooking Time: 5 mins

Goat Cheese Pastries
Briwattes Ba Jben

For a delicious variation: sweeten the goat's cheese with sugar to taste, blend it with $^1/_4$ cup (60 g) melted butter, 1 tablespoon crème fraîche or heavy cream, and 1 teaspoon orange flower water. Follow the recipe but omit the eggs.

8 oz (250 g) fresh goat cheese
$^1/_4$ cup (60 g) butter
Pinch each of salt and freshly ground
  black pepper
2 tablespoons fresh thyme leaves
1 egg, lightly beaten
5 sheets filo pastry or Warka Pastry
  Leaf (page 35)
Oil for deep-frying

1 Combine the goat cheese, the butter, salt, pepper, thyme, and beaten egg in a bowl and mix well.
2 Cut each sheet of filo into four long strips, place a spoonful of the seasoned goat cheese at one short end, fold the corner down to form a triangle, then continue folding at right angles. To seal the triangle, tuck the end into the last fold like an envelope (page 35).
3 In a large pan, heat the oil over medium heat. Deep-fry the pastries until golden, about 3–4 minutes, turning them regularly. Drain on paper towels and serve hot.

Preparation Time: 45 mins
Cooking Time: 5 mins

Rolls Scented with Nigella Seeds

$1^1/_2$ teaspoons active dried yeast
$^1/_4$ cup (60 ml) warm water
2 cups (300 g) flour
$^1/_2$ cup (75 g) fine semolina flour
$^1/_2$ teaspoon nigella seeds
$^1/_2$ teaspoon salt
2 teaspoons sugar
$^1/_4$ cup (60 g) butter, melted
1 egg, lightly beaten
1 egg yolk, lightly beaten

1 Dissolve the yeast in a little of the warm water and set it aside.
2 Combine the flours and the nigella seeds, salt and sugar in a large bowl and mix well. Make a well in the center and add the melted butter and the beaten egg and mix in. Add the dissolved yeast and knead into a soft dough, regularly sprinkling it with more water if it's too dry.
3 Divide the dough into six equal pieces. Sprinkle each piece with 1 tablespoon of flour, place on a cloth, cover loosely and set aside to rise for 1 hour in a warm place.
4 Preheat the oven to 400°F (200°C). Flatten the balls of dough and place them on a baking sheet. Brush the tops with egg yolk and prick each roll a few times with a fork. Bake for 10 minutes or until golden.

Preparation Time: 30 mins + $1^1/_2$ hours for dough to rest
Cooking Time: 10 mins

Shrimp Pastries

2 tablespoons oil
3 cloves garlic, peeled and crushed
   with a little water to form a paste
3 tablespoons chopped fresh
   coriander leaves (cilantro)
$1/2$ teaspoon salt
Pinch of ground cumin
Juice of $1/2$ lemon
1 tomato, peeled, deseeded, and
   finely diced
8 oz (250 g) fresh shrimp, peeled
1 green finger-length chili pepper
   (optional)
6 sheets filo pastry or Warka Pastry
   Leaf (page 35)
1 egg yolk
Oil for deep-frying

1 Heat 2 tablespoons of oil in a pan over medium heat and sauté the garlic, cilantro, salt, cumin, and lemon juice for 3 minutes. Reduce the heat, add the tomato and cook for 7 minutes. Add the shrimp and chili (if using) and cook for another 3–4 minutes, remove from heat and cool.

2 Cut the sheets of filo in half. In the middle of each sheet, place 1 tablespoon of filling, fold in both sides, then roll to form cigar shapes. Seal and brush with egg yolk.

3 In a large pan, heat the oil over medium–high heat. Deep-fry the pastries until golden, about 5 minutes. Serve hot.

Preparation Time: 30 mins
Cooking Time: 20 mins

Spiced Meat Pastries

2 cups (300 g) flour
$1/2$ teaspoon salt
1 cup (250 ml) water
5 tablespoons olive oil
8 oz (250 g) ground beef
2 cloves garlic, minced
1 teaspoon ground cumin
1 teaspoon ground coriander

1 Sift the flour into a mixing bowl with a pinch of the salt. Add the water, 2 tablespoons of the oil, and knead until dough is elastic. Set aside to rest for 20 minutes.

2 Heat the remaining oil in a skillet and sauté the ground beef, garlic, and spices. Cook until the beef is uniformly brown and set aside to cool.

3 Divide the dough into approximately ten pieces. Roll each piece into a $1 1/2$-in (40-mm) ball. Flatten each one on an oiled surface to form a disk. Place 1 teaspoon of filling on each disk and fold in the sides to form a square. Brush the top of each pastry with oil and set aside.

4 Heat the skillet over medium heat and brown the pastries, 3 minutes each side.

Preparation Time: 30 mins + 20 mins
   for dough to rest
Cooking Time: 30 mins

BELOW: Crisp-fried pastries with sweet and savory fillings are served as appetizers or snacks.

Moroccan Chicken Pie B'stilla

3 tablespoons olive oil
4 large onions, peeled and sliced
1 teaspoon *ras el hanout* (page 32)
1 free-range chicken (about 2¹/₄
  lbs/1kg), quartered
1 cup (250 ml) water
¹/₄ cup (60 ml) fresh lemon juice
1 small bunch fresh coriander leaves
  (cilantro), chopped
1 small bunch flat-leaf parsley,
  chopped

Almond Paste
1¹/₂ cups (225 g) blanched, peeled
  almonds
2 tablespoons oil
¹/₂ cup (100 g) sugar
¹/₂ teaspoon ground cinnamon
1 tablespoon orange flower water

Pastry
12 sheets filo pastry or Warka Pastry
  Leaf (page 35)
³/₄ cup (180 g) butter, melted
2 egg yolks, lightly beaten

Toppings (optional)
³/₄ cup (100 g) confectioners' sugar
1 teaspoon ground cinnamon

1 Preheat the oven to 350°F (175°C). Heat the oil over medium–high heat in a large Dutch oven. Add the onions, the *ras el hanout* and mix well. Add the chicken and brown it on all sides. Add the water, cover and bake in the oven for 45 minutes or until the chicken is cooked.

2 Remove the chicken from the pot and set it aside to cool. Add the lemon juice to the sauce and reduce it on top of the stove over medium heat for 10 minutes. While the sauce is cooking, strip the meat off the bones, cut it into small pieces and set it aside.

3 To make the Almond Paste, heat the oil in a skillet and fry the almonds until golden, taking care not to burn them. Remove the almonds from the pan and process them in a food processor until finely ground. Combine the almonds with the sugar, cinnamon, and orange flower water in a bowl. Stir or knead until the mixture is a thick paste.

4 Grease a 9-in (23-cm), round baking dish with butter. Lay one sheet of pastry in the center of the dish and brush with butter. Fan additional sheets of pastry out from the center of the dish and brush each sheet with butter. Layer half of the Almond Paste in the dish, cover with the chicken, then the sauce. Top with the remaining Almond Paste. Layer three sheets of pastry over the top and make a seam by tucking the overhang under the edge of the inside of the dish. Brush the top of the pie with the remaining melted butter and brush the pastry seams with beaten egg yolk.

5 Bake for 1 hour at 400°F (200°C). Serve the pie sprinkled with confectioners' sugar and cinnamon, if desired.

Serves 6–8   Preparation time: 1¹/₂ hours   Cooking time: 1¹/₂ hours

Moroccan Seafood Pie   Seafood B'stilla

2 lbs (1 kg) fresh mussels, washed
3 tablespoons olive oil
3 cloves garlic, peeled and crushed
2 medium-sized tomatoes, peeled
  and diced
1 onion, peeled and cut into thick
  slices
1 lemon, cut in half, one half juiced
  and the other diced (with peel on)
1 teaspoon salt
$1/2$ teaspoon freshly ground black
  pepper
$1/2$ teaspoon paprika
$1/2$ teaspoon ground cumin
10 oz (300 g) mushrooms, wiped
  clean and sliced
2 carrots, peeled and grated
7 oz (200 g) fresh squid, cut in strips
7 oz (200 g) fresh cod or other flaky
  white fish fillets, cut in large chunks
12 oz (350 g) fresh medium-sized
  shrimp, washed
$1/2$ cup (125 g) butter, melted
12 sheets filo pastry or Warka Pastry
  Leaf (page 35)
1 small bunch fresh coriander leaves
  (cilantro), chopped
1 small bunch flat-leaf parsley,
  chopped
1 egg yolk

Garnishes
6 black olives
$1/2$ lemon, sliced

1 Place the mussels and 1 cup (250 ml) of water in a large pot. Cover and steam over high heat for 7–9 minutes or until they open. Remove the meats and discard the shells as well as any unopened mussels. Set aside in a mixing bowl.

2 In the same pot, heat the oil and add the garlic, tomatoes, onion, lemon juice, diced lemon, salt, pepper, paprika, cumin, mushrooms and grated carrots. Cook over medium–high heat, covered, for 5–8 minutes.
Add the squid and continue to cook for 10 minutes; add the fish and shrimp and cook for another 10 minutes. Turn off the heat and remove the shrimp. Set aside about 18 shrimp for garnish, two-thirds of them peeled, the rest left unpeeled. Peel the remaining shrimp and return them to the pot with the chopped herbs and mix well.

3 Grease a 9-in (23-cm) baking dish with butter. Place one sheet of pastry in the bottom of the dish and fan another 4 sheets out from the center, extending out over the edge of the dish. Fill the dish half-full with the seafood mixture, drained of its sauce. Fold the overhanging pastry towards the middle, and cover with a second layer of filling. Cover with the remaining pastry sheets and form a seam by folding the pastry over the edges and tucking inside the rim of the dish. Seal the seams with egg yolk.

4 Bake the pie for 20 minutes at 400°F (200°C). Serve garnished with the reserved shrimp, olives, and sliced lemon.

Serves 6   Preparation time: 1 hour   Cooking time: 1 hour

Moroccan Caraway Soup   Harira

This soup, called *Harira* is the star of Ramadan for it is with this divine soup that the daily fast is broken.

1 lb (500 g) boneless lamb, cubed
2 onions, peeled and minced
$^2/_3$ cup (100 g) dried chickpeas,
    soaked in cold, salted water
    overnight, then drained
1 heaping tablespoon green lentils
$^1/_2$ cup (100 g) dried fava beans,
    soaked, drained and peeled
1 bunch flat-leaf parsley, chopped
1 small stalk celery, chopped
2 teaspoons salt
1 cinnamon stick
1 teaspoon each: ground ginger,
    ground black pepper, paprika,
    ground cumin, and ground turmeric
4 cups (1 liter) beef stock or water
One 28-oz (800-g) can tomato purée
3 tablespoons tomato paste
1 bunch fresh coriander leaves
    (cilantro), finely chopped
1 teaspoon caraway seeds

Garnishes
2 lemons, cut in wedges
12 dates

1 Combine the lamb, onions, chickpeas, lentils, fava beans, parsley, celery, and salt in a large stockpot. Add the spices, cover with the stock or water and bring to a boil. Reduce the heat and simmer for $1^1/_2$ hours.
2 When the chickpeas are soft, add the tomato puree, tomato paste, fresh coriander leaves, and the caraway seeds. Cook for another 5 minutes.
3 Serve garnished with wedges of lemon and dates.

Note: For a delicious alternative, add $3^1/_2$ oz (100 g) cubed *jben* or mild goat cheese, 2 beaten eggs, and a pinch of salt and pepper once the chickpeas are cooked.

Serves 8
Preparation time: Overnight to soak the chickpeas +1 hour
Cooking time: 2 hours

Fava Bean Soup   Bissara

Bissara is a pauper's dish that has become the food of kings. It can be served as a first course or as a soup with the evening meal.

1 tablespoons olive oil
2 cups (300 g) dried fava beans
3 cloves garlic, peeled and crushed
$^1/_2$ teaspoon ground cumin
$^1/_2$ teaspoon paprika
1 teaspoons salt
4 cups (1 liter) water

Garnishes
$^1/_2$ teaspoon ground cumin
$^1/_2$ teaspoon paprika
2 teaspoons olive oil

1 In a large pot, heat the oil over medium heat. Add the beans, garlic, cumin, paprika, salt and water and cook, uncovered, for 1 hour, stirring occasionally.
2 When the beans are cooked, put the mixture through a food mill, then reheat for a few minutes. Serve hot or cold, with a sprinkling of cumin, paprika, and a drizzle of olive oil.

Serves 4   Preparation time: 15 mins   Cooking time: 1 hour

Wild Thyme Potatoes

This simple dish is surprisingly tasty and can be prepared very quickly.

1 small bunch wild thyme
2 teaspoons olive oil
1 small onion, peeled and thinly
  sliced
$^1/_2$ teaspoon salt
Pinch of ground white pepper
1 cup (250 ml) water
$1^1/_2$ lbs (750 g) new potatoes or
  other firm, waxy potatoes, cut into
  pieces
1 medium-sized tomato, peeled and
  sliced

1 Quickly rinse the thyme, reserve a few whole sprigs for the garnish, and remove the flowers and leaves from the other sprigs.
2 In a large pot, preferably cast iron, heat the oil and sauté the onion for 5 to 7 minutes until golden. Add salt, pepper, and water and bring to a boil. Add the potatoes and tomatoes, cover, reduce the heat, and cook for 10 minutes. Add the thyme leaves and flowers, cover again, and cook for another 15 minutes. Taste and correct the seasoning, if necessary.
3 Transfer the potatoes and the sauce to serving dish. Serve garnished with the reserved thyme.

Serves 4   Preparation time: 20 mins   Cooking time: 30 mins

Spring Vegetable Couscous

1 lb (500 g) baby zucchinis, blossoms attached if possible
1 onion, peeled and quartered
1 teaspoon salt
$^1/_2$ teaspoon ground white pepper
$^1/_2$ teaspoon ground ginger
$^1/_4$ teaspoon saffron threads
Harissa or other hot pepper paste, to taste (optional)
1 bunch fresh coriander leaves (cilantro)
6 cups (1$^1/_2$ liters) water
3 tablespoons olive oil
1$^1/_2$ cups (250 g) fresh shelled fava beans (or 7 oz/200 g frozen lima beans)
1$^1/_2$ cups (250 g) fresh shelled peas (or 5 oz/150 g frozen peas)
1 portion prepared Couscous (page 34)

1 Wash the zucchini, reserve six for the garnish, and cut the others in quarters.
2 Combine the onion, salt, spices, coriander leaves and water in a large pot. Bring to a boil, taste and adjustt the seasoning. And the oil, beans, peas, and zucchini, reduce the heat to low and simmer for 20 minutes.
3 Meanwhile, cook the couscous according to the instructions on page 34. To serve, make a dome of couscous in a large, shallow earthenware dish. Flatten the top of the dome and place the vegetables in the middle. Pour the stock over the vegetables.

Note: *Harissa* is a mixture of red peppers and spices that can overpower the subtle flavors of this vegetable couscous. You can omit it if you don't like spicy food.

Serves 6   Preparation time: 30 mins   Cooking time: 30 mins

Herb Stuffed Chicken

1 free-range chicken, cleaned and dried
$1/_2$ teaspoon salt
8 cups (2 liters) water
2 bay leaves
3 carrots, peeled
3 onions, peeled
6 medium potatoes, peeled
1 bunch fresh coriander leaves (cilantro)
1 bunch flat-leaf parsley

Stuffing
1 bunch fresh coriander leaves (cilantro), finely chopped
1 bunch flat-leaf parsley, finely chopped
4 cloves garlic, peeled and crushed
1 onion, peeled and thinly sliced
1 teaspoon salt
1 teaspoon ground pepper
1 teaspoon ground cumin
1 teaspoon paprika

Accompaniments
1 teaspoon ground cumin
1 teaspoon salt

1 To prepare the Stuffing, combine all the ingredients in a bowl, mix well, and set aside.
2 Rub the skin of the chicken with the salt, fill the cavity with the Stuffing and sew the opening shut using a large needle and thread.
3 In the bottom of a steamer, heat the water with the bay leaves. In the basket of the steamer, place the chicken, the whole vegetables, and the herbs. Cover and steam for 1 hour over simmering water.
4 Discard the herbs. Halve the carrots lengthwise and cut the onions and potatos into bite-sized pieces. To serve, place the chicken in the middle of a large serving dish with the vegetables arranged around it. Serve with small bowls of ground cumin and salt to sprinkle over the chicken meat to taste.

Note: Wild Thyme Potatoes (page 49) are very good paired with this dish.

Serves 6   Preparation time: 30 mins   Cooking time: 1 hour

Roast Chicken with Lemon Sauce

1 free-range chicken, cleaned and dried
2 heaping teaspoons nigella seeds, 1 teaspoon crushed, the other left whole
6 tablespoons olive oil
2 onions, peeled and thinly sliced
Pinch of ground ginger
1 teaspoon salt
Pinch of freshly ground black pepper
2 cups (500 ml) water
Several saffron threads
1 bunch fresh coriander leaves (cilantro)
1 large Preserved Lemon (page 35), quartered

1 Rub the chicken with 1 teaspoon of crushed nigella seeds. Heat the oil in a pot large enough to fit the chicken. Add the onions, ginger, salt, pepper and chicken. Brown the chicken on all sides over high heat, about 5 minutes. Add the water and saffron and bring to a boil. Add the chopped coriander, the whole nigella seeds, and Preserved Lemon. Cover, reduce the heat and and simmer until the chicken is cooked, about 40 minutes.
2 Transfer the chicken to a serving dish and pour the sauce from the pot over it, ensuring that it is covered with seeds and lemon pieces. Serve hot.

Nigella seeds are very fragrant when crushed. A mortar and pestle works best, but you can also crush them in a bowl with the back of a spoon.

Serves 6   Preparation time: 20 mins   Cooking time: 45 mins

Fragrant Spiced Chicken with Olives

1 free-range chicken, cleaned, dried and cut into large pieces
4 tablespoons olive oil
$^1/_2$ teaspoon salt
Pinch of freshly ground black pepper
Pinch of ground ginger
Pinch of saffron threads
1 stick cinnamon or $^1/_2$ teaspoon ground cinnamon
1 onion, peeled and thinly sliced
1 tomato, peeled, deseeded and chopped
1 bunch flat-leaf parsley, chopped
1 bunch fresh coriander leaves (cilantro), chopped
4 cloves garlic, whole
2 cups (500 ml) water
1 cup (250 g) pitted olives
1 Preserved Lemon (page 35), sliced

1 Heat the oil in a large, heavy pot. Add the chicken, salt, spices, and
onion, and cook for 7 minutes, turning the meat to brown it evenly. Add the
tomato, herbs, whole garlic cloves and the water and bring to a boil.
Reduce the heat and simmer for 45 minutes.
2 When the meat is cooked, take a ladle of stock from the pot and heat it in
a small saucepan with the olives and lemon. Reduce the stock for at least
five minutes, then remove from the heat.
3 To serve, arrange the chicken on a serving platter, cover with the reduced
sauce, olives, and sliced lemon. Serve with fresholy baked Moroccan bread
(page 37).

Serves 6   Preparation time: 30 mins   Cooking time: 1 hour

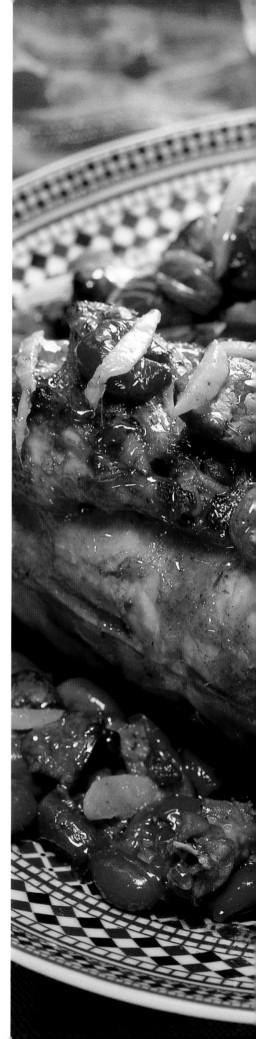

Chicken with Eggplant and Fresh Herbs

1 onion, peeled and thinly sliced
1 free-range chicken, cleaned, dried and cut into 8 pieces
1 cup (250 ml) water
1 whole bulb of garlic, left whole
3 tablespoons olive oil
1 teaspoon salt
1 teaspoon freshly ground black pepper
1 teaspoon ground cinnamon
1 teaspoon paprika
1 bunch flat-leaf parsley, chopped
1 bunch fresh coriander leaves (cilantro), chopped
Oil for deep-frying
2 lbs (1 kg) globe eggplants, sliced into $3/4$-in (2-cm) rounds, sprinkled with salt
  and allowed to sweat then dried with paper towels

Garnish
1 Preserved Lemon (page 35), sliced

1 Combine the onion, chicken, water, whole bulb of garlic, oil, salt, spices, and herbs in a large pot and bring to a boil. Reduce the heat and simmer, covered, for 45 minutes.
2 Heat the oil in a deep pan and deep-fry the eggplant slices. Remove them and drain on paper towels. Slice the eggplant into thin strips.
3 Arrange the chicken on a serving platter, make a little nest of eggplant strips on top of each piece of chicken, then garnish with slices of Preserved Lemon.

Serves 6   Preparation time: 30 mins   Cooking time: 1 hour

Chicken with Marinated Figs and Walnuts

2 tablespoons olive oil
1 free-range chicken, cleaned, dried and cut into 8 pieces
2 onions, peeled and sliced
2 cloves garlic, peeled and crushed
$1/_2$ teaspoon ground ginger
$1/_2$ teaspoon salt
Several saffron threads
1 bunch fresh coriander leaves (cilantro), chopped
1 cup (250 ml) water
10 tablespoons butter
2 tablespoons honey

Marinated Figs
1 teaspoon ground cinnamon
$1/_2$ teaspoon ground ginger
$1/_2$ teaspoon nutmeg
$1/_2$ teaspoon freshly ground black pepper
$1/_2$ teaspoon salt
1 tablespoon water
1 lb (500 g) fresh figs, washed and sliced

Garnish
1 cup (250 g) shelled raw walnuts, halved

1 To prepare the Marinated Figs, combine the spices, salt, and water in a mixing bowl. Add the figs, toss gently, and set aside to marinate for 1 hour.
2 Combine the oil, chicken, onions, garlic, ginger, salt, saffron, and chopped coriander leaves in a large Dutch oven or pot. Add the water, bring to a boil, then reduce the heat and simmer for 45 minutes, stirring occasionally.
3 Melt 5 tablespoons of butter in a skillet. Drain the figs, add them to the pan with the honey and cook gently for 7 minutes.
4 Melt the remaining 5 tablespoons of butter in another skillet. Drain the chicken and brown each piece over medium heat.
5 To serve, arrange the chicken on a platter and pour the warm cooking juices over the top. Garnish with the figs and sprinkle with walnut halves.

Serves 6   Preparation time: 20 mins   Cooking time: 1 hour 15 mins

Chicken with Apricot Sauce and Pine Nuts

1 free-range chicken, cleaned, dried and cut into serving pieces
4 tablespoons olive oil
1 teaspoon salt
$1/_2$ teaspoon freshly ground black pepper
$1/_4$ teaspoon ground ginger
Pinch of saffron threads
1 stick cinnamon
2 small onions, peeled and thinly sliced
1 cup (250 ml) water
$1/_2$ cup (125 g) pine nuts, dry roasted in a pan until golden

Apricot Sauce
1 lb (500 g) fresh apricots, peeled and halved
1 cup (250 ml) water
$1/_2$ cup (100 g) sugar
1 teaspoon cinnamon
$1/_2$ cup (125 g) butter

1 To prepare the Apricot Sauce, place the apricots in a saucepan with the water, sugar, cinnamon and butter, and bring to a boil. Reduce the heat to low and cook, uncovered, until the liquid has reduced to a syrup consistency.
2 Heat the oil in a pot big enough to fit the chicken pieces. Add the chicken pieces and brown them. Season with the salt, pepper, ginger, and saffron and add the cinnamon stick. Add the onions and water and simmer, covered, for 30 minutes.
3 To serve, arrange the chicken and the apricots on a serving platter. Drizzle with the sauce and garnish the roasted pine nuts.

Serves 6   Preparation time: 30 mins   Cooking time: 45 mins

Roast Pigeon Stuffed with Almonds and Couscous

$^2/_3$ cup (120 g) raisins
2 cups (500 ml) water
1 tablespoon orange flower water
$1^1/_2$ cups (250 g) dried couscous
5 tablespoons salted butter
$^1/_2$ cup (100 g) blanched and peeled almonds, sautéed in oil until golden,
  then chopped
Pinch of ground nutmeg
$^1/_2$ teaspoon saffron threads
1 tablespoon honey
6 pigeons or Cornish hens, cleaned
2 onions, peeled and cut in thick slices
3 tablespoons olive oil
1 teaspoon salt
$^1/_2$ teaspoon ground white pepper
$^1/_2$ teaspoon ground ginger
3 cloves
2 cinnamon sticks
2 cups (500 ml) water

1 Soak the raisins in 2 cups (500 ml) of water and 1 tablespoon of orange flower water for 1 hour. Drain well.
2 Prepare the couscous according to the instructions on page 34. Combine the couscous, the butter, chopped almonds, drained raisins, nutmeg, saffron, and honey in a large bowl and mix well. Stuff the pigeons or Cornish hens with half of the mixture and sew them shut using a large needle and thread.
3 Combine the onions and 3 tablespoons of olive oil in a large pot. Place the pigeons or Cornish hens on top. Season with salt and pepper and the remaining spices and add 2 cups (500 ml) of water. Cover and cook over high heat for a few minutes. Reduce the heat and cook for 1 hour. Add an additional $^1/_2$ cup (125 ml) of water during cooking, if needed.
4 To serve, remove the thread from the pigeons and arrange them on a serving dish. Serve with the additional couscous.

Serves 6   Preparation time: 1 hour   Cooking time: 1 hour

Braised Lamb with Peas and Artichokes

2 lbs (1 kg) boneless lamb, cut into 2-in (5-cm) cubes
2 onions, peeled and sliced thinly
2 cloves garlic, peeled and crushed
2 tablespoons olive oil
1 teaspoon salt
2 cups (500 ml) water
$1/2$ teaspoon paprika
$1/4$ teaspoon ground ginger
$1/4$ teaspoon ground pepper
1 lb (500 g) fresh artichokes (see Helpful Hint below)
1 lemon, one half juiced the other half cut into quarters
3 cups (500 g) fresh shelled or thawed frozen peas

1 Combine the lamb, onions, garlic, oil, and salt in a large pan. Sauté for 3–4 minutes to brown the meat evenly. Add the water and the spices, turn the heat to high and bring to a boil. Reduce the heat and simmer, covered, for 1 hour.
2 While the meat is cooking, prepare the artichokes by breaking off the stems and removing the tough outer leaves. Trim off the top two-thirds, and remove the fuzzy choke, then drop into a mixing bowl filled with water, the juice of half a lemon and the lemon wedges. This will prevent the artichokes from discoloring.
3 Add the peas to the stew and cook for 5 minutes. Add the artichokes and simmer for another 15 minutes.
4 To serve, first arrange the meat in a dish, then the artichokes and peas, and finally add the sauce and serve with freshly baked Moroccan bread (page 37).

Note: Try to look for the small poivrade variety of artichokes. If you use the large globe variety, remove the outer leaves, clean, and quarter them.

Serves 4   Preparation time: 45 mins   Cooking time: $1^1/2$ hours

Lamb with Chestnuts and Cinnamon

This recipe originates from Tlemcen, a pretty Algerian town some 50 miles (80 km) from the Moroccan border. If you are using dried chestnuts, you must wash and soak them in cold water the day before you intend to cook them. Alternatively, use vacuum-packed or canned chestnuts which do not need to be presoaked and are faster to cook.

3 tablespoons olive oil
2^1/$_2$ lbs (1^1/$_4$ kg) boneless lamb shoulder, cut into serving pieces
2 onions, peeled and thinly sliced
^{1}/$_2$ teaspoon salt
^{1}/$_4$ teaspoon saffron threads
^{1}/$_4$ teaspoon ground nutmeg
1 stick cinnamon, broken in two
1 cup (250 ml) water
14 oz (400 g) dried chestnuts, presoaked overnight and drained or 1 lb (500 g) vacuum-packed or canned chestnuts
1 tablespoon sugar
1 tablespoon orange flower water (page 32)

1 In a large pot, heat the oil, then add the meat and brown for a minute or two. Add the onions, salt, spices and water, stir, and bring to a boil.
If using presoaked dried chestnuts, add them to the pan now, reduce the heat and simmer for 45 minutes. If using vacuum-packed or canned chestnuts, cook the meat for 30 minutes before adding the chestnuts. Add an extra ^{1}/$_2$ cup (125 ml) of water if the sauce has evaporated. The chestnuts should be soft and the meat tender.
2 Add the sugar and the orange flower water. Reduce the sauce over low heat until it thickens.
3 To serve, arrange the meat in a serving dish, cover with the chestnuts, and pour the sauce over the top.

Serves 6   Preparation time: 20 mins   Cooking time: 1 hour

Lamb Stuffed with Couscous and Dates

1 teaspoon salt
1 shoulder of lamb, about 3 lbs (1$^1/_2$ kg), deboned and butterflied
$^1/_4$ teaspoon saffron threads
$^1/_2$ teaspoon freshly ground black pepper
1 tablespoon butter
2$^1/_2$ tablespoons salted butter

Stuffing
$^1/_2$ cup (125 g) raisins
1 tablespoon orange flower water (page 32)
1$^1/_4$ cups (250 g) cooked couscous (page 34)
$^1/_2$ cup (125 g) butter, melted
$^1/_2$ cup (125 g) sugar
1 teaspoon ground cinnamon
$^3/_4$ cup (190 g) almonds, peeled and chopped
1 cup (250 g) dates, pitted and diced

Garnish
6–8 raw peeled almonds, toasted
6–8 fresh dates, pitted

1 Rub the lamb with the salt and steam in a steamer for 1 hour, checking regularly that the water has not completely evaporated.
2 To prepare the Stuffing, soak the raisins in water with $^1/_2$ tablespoon of the orange flower water for 15 minutes. Combine the couscous, melted butter, soaked raisins, sugar, cinnamon, chopped almonds, dates, and the remaining orange flower water and mix well. Set aside.
3 Preheat the oven to 350°F (180°C). Combine the saffron, pepper and butter in a bowl. Remove the meat from the steamer and stuff it with the Stuffing. Using a needle and strong cooking thread, sew the opening shut. Coat the lamb with the seasoned butter and roast it for 30 minutes in the oven.
4 Prepare the Garnish by stuffing each pitted date with a toasted almond. To serve, place the roasted lamb on a serving platter, then cut the thread so some of the stuffing spills out. Garnish with the stuffed dates.

Note: Use a colored thread to sew the meat so it is easier to locate when carving.

Serves 6   Preparation time: 1 hour   Cooking time: 1$^1/_2$ hours

Lamb Confit with Raisins and Almonds

$^1/_2$ teaspoon salt
1 pinch saffron threads
2 teaspoons *ras el hanout* spice mix (page 32)
4 cups (1 liter) water
6 lamb shanks, or 6 pieces lamb shoulder
2 tablespoons olive oil
2 onions, peeled and thinly sliced
$2^1/_2$ tablespoons salted butter
1 cup (250 g) blanched and peeled almonds
2 cups (300 g) golden raisins or currants
$^1/_2$ cup (125 ml) honey
$^1/_3$ cup (40 g) sesame seeds, toasted

1 Combine the salt, saffron, *ras el hanout* spice mix and 1 cup (250 ml) of the water in a bowl and mix well. Rub the meat with half of this spice mixture. Reserve the remaining spice mixture for later.
2 Place the meat in a large pot together with the oil, the remaining 3 cups (750 ml) of water, the onions, butter and almonds. Cook, covered, over low heat for 2 hours. Check the liquid from time to time and add a little water if necessary.
3 Meanwhile, soak the raisins or currants in warm water. After two hours, drain and add them to the meat, along with the reserved spice mixture. Cook for 20 minutes, then add the honey and continue to cook, uncovered, until the raisins and the almonds start to caramelize.
4 Serve hot, garnished with the toasted sesame seeds and with freshly baked Moroccan bread (page 37).

Serves 6   Preparation time: 30 mins   Cooking time: $2^1/_2$ hours

Lamb with Zucchini and Fresh Mint

2 tablespoons olive oil
2 lbs (1 kg) boneless lamb shoulder, cut into 6 pieces
1 stick cinnamon
Large pinch saffron threads
$^1/_4$ teaspoon freshly ground black pepper
$^1/_2$ teaspoon salt
3 cloves garlic, peeled and crushed
2 cups (500 ml) water
Oil for deep-frying
2 lbs (1 kg) zucchini, ends removed, washed, dried and thinly sliced
$^1/_2$ teaspoon salt
Pinch of ground pepper
1 bunch mint leaves, washed and chopped (keep a few leaves whole for garnish)

1 Heat the oil in a large pot and add the meat, cinnamon stick, saffron, pepper, salt, and garlic. Turn the meat to brown it evenly. Pour the water around the meat (not directly over it). Bring to a boil, reduce the heat and simmer, covered, for 45 minutes. Taste and adjust the seasoning if necessary.
2 Heat the oil for deep-frying in a pan and deep-fry the zucchini slices. Remove and drain on paper towels.
3 Serve the meat with the slices of zucchini on top. Sprinkle with salt, pepper and chopped mint leaves. Garnish with whole mint leaves.

Serves 6   Preparation time: 30 mins   Cooking time: 1 hour

Lamb with Prunes and Sesame Seeds

3 lbs (1¹/₂ kg) boneless lamb shoulder, cut into serving pieces
5 tablespoons olive oil
1 stick cinnamon
1 pinch saffron threads
¹/₂ teaspoon freshly ground black pepper
2 onions, peeled and thinly sliced
1 teaspoon salt
2 cups (500 ml)
12 oz (350 g) dried prunes
¹/₂ cup (125 g) sugar
1 teaspoon ground cinnamon
¹/₂ cup (125 g) butter
¹/₂ cup (125 ml) water

Garnishes
1¹/₄ cups (300 g) raw almonds, toasted (see Note)
Handful of toasted sesame seeds

1 Place the meat in a large pot with the oil, cinnamon stick, saffron, pepper, and onions. Add the salt, cover with the water and bring to a boil. Reduce the heat and simmer for 1 hour. When the meat is cooked, remove it from the pot, cover it and set it aside.
2 Remove the cinnamon stick from the pot and discard it. Add the prunes, sugar, ground cinnamon, butter, and ¹/₂ cup (125 ml) of water and mix well. Simmer, covered, until the sauce thickens to a syrup consistency.
3 Return the meat to the pot along with any juice it has released and simmer for 15 minutes.
4 Serve garnished with toasted sesame seeds and a sprinkling of almonds.

Note: Toast the almonds and sesame seeds in separate batches. Place the nuts or seeds in a dry skillet over medium heat and stir continuously. The nuts and seeds are toasted when they are golden and fragrant (almonds take about 5 minutes and sesame seeds should toast more quickly). Remove them from the skillet immediately to prevent them from burning.

Serves 6   Preparation time: 30 mins   Cooking time: 1¹/₂ hours

Braised Lamb with Fava Beans

$2^1/_2$ lbs ($1^1/_4$ kg) boneless lamb shoulder, cut into serving pieces
1 teaspoon salt
$^1/_2$ teaspoon freshly ground black pepper
3 tablespoons olive oil
3 cloves garlic, peeled and crushed with a little water to form a paste
2 cups (500 ml) water
$^1/_2$ teaspoon cumin
$^1/_2$ teaspoon paprika
$1^1/_2$ lbs (680 g) fresh fava beans, shelled or 1 lb (500 g) frozen shelled beans

1 Season the meat with the salt and pepper. Heat the oil in a large pot and brown the meat for 5 minutes. Add the garlic, water, and spices. Bring to a boil, then reduce the heat and simmer for 35 minutes, uncovered.
2 Add the beans and cook for 20 minutes. Remove from the heat. Arrange the meat on a platter. Add the sauce and the beans.

Serves 6   Preparation time: 30 mins   Cooking time: 1 hour

Lamb with Onions and Cinnamon

3 tablespoons olive oil
1 medium-sized tomato, peeled and sliced
$2^1/_2$ lbs ($1^1/_4$ kg) boneless lamb, cut into large pieces
1 teaspoon salt
3 sticks cinnamon
$^1/_2$ teaspoon saffron threads
$^1/_2$ teaspoon ground white pepper
2 lbs (1 kg) small onions, peeled and sliced into thick rings
2 cups (500 ml) water
$^1/_2$ teaspoon ground cinnamon

1 Combine the olive oil, tomato, lamb, salt, and spices—except the ground cinnamon—in a tagine or large cast iron pot (see Note). Place the onions on top of the meat and add the water. Cover and cook over low heat for 1 hour ($1^1/_2$ hours if you are using a cast iron pot).
2 Taste and correct the seasoning. Serve directly from the tagine or arrange the meat on a serving platter. Cover it with the sauce, then garnish with the onions. Sprinkle the ground cinnamon over the top of ths dish.

Note: An earthenware tagine is best for this recipe. If you do not have one, use a cast iron pot.

Serves 4   Preparation time: 30 mins   Cooking time: 1 hour

Lamb with Caramelized Onions and Raisins

2 lbs (1 kg) boneless lamb, cut into bite-sized pieces
4 medium onions, peeled and finely chopped
$^1/_2$ teaspoon ground ginger
3 sticks cinnamon
4 cloves
$^1/_2$ teaspoon freshly ground black pepper
1 teaspoon salt
1 bunch fresh coriander leaves (cilantro)
1 bunch flat-leaf parsley
6 cups ($1^1/_2$ liters) water
1 portion prepared Couscous (page 34)
1 cup (150 g) golden raisins or currants
2 tablespoons orange flower water (page 32)
2 tablespoons salted butter
1 tablespoon sugar
1 teaspoon ground cinnamon
2 pinches ground saffron

Garnishes
$^3/_4$ cup (200 g) raw almonds, browned in oil and chopped
3 hard-boiled eggs, halved

1 Place the meat, onions, ginger, cinnamon sticks, cloves, pepper, salt, coriander leaves, parsley and water in a pot. Bring to a boil and simmer, uncovered, for 30 minutes. Taste and adjust the seasoning as necessary.
2 Prepare the Couscous by following the instructions on page 34.
Soak the raisins for about 10 minutes in cold water with 1 tablespoon of the orange flower water.
3 Remove the onions, herbs, and a smll amount of liquid from the pot to a heavy pan and add the butter, sugar, remaining orange flower water and ground cinnamon then saute until the onions begin to caramelize. Add the raisins and cook for 10 minutes until all the water has evaporated. Discard the herbs.
4 To serve, spoon the couscous around the edge of a serving platter and place the meat in the center. Top the couscous with the raisins and the onions. Ladle a little stock over the top and garnish with chopped almonds and hard-boiled egg halves. Serve the remaining gravy in a tureen for guests to drizzle over the couscous.

Serves 4   Preparation time: 45 mins   Cooking time: 45 mins

Lamb with Quince and Cinnamon

3 lbs (1$^1/_2$ kg) boneless lamb shouler, cut into 8–12 pieces
$^1/_2$ cup (120 g) butter
1 stick cinnamon
4 teaspoons ground ginger
Pinch of saffron threads
1 onion, peeled and thinly sliced
$^1/_2$ teaspoon salt
2 lbs (1 kg) ripe quinces or Granny Smith apples, halved, cored and deseeded
3 tablespoons honey
1 teaspoon ground cinnamon
1 cup (250 ml) water
1 lb (500 g) okra, stems removed

1 Combine the lamb, butter, cinnamon, ginger, saffron, onion, and salt in a tagine or a large pot. Add enough water to cover the meat, and cook over low heat for 1 hour. When the meat is done, remove it from the pot and keep covered.
2 Remove the cinnamon stick from the pot of liquid and discard it. Add the quinces or apples to the pot together with the honey, cinnamon and water. Stir gently, bring to a boil and simmer, covered, until the quinces are tender, about 15 minutes.
3 Return the meat to the pot, along with any juices it released, add the okra and cook for 10 minutes, taking care not to overcook the okra. Serve with freshly baked Moroccan bread (page 37).

Serves 6   Preparation time: 30 mins   Cooking time: 1$^1/_2$ hours

Roast Leg of Lamb Mechoui

There are numerous ways to prepare a *mechoui*. Townsfolk in Morocco generally take the meat to the local baker to be cooked in his oven but traditionally it is roasted on a spit in the open air. A large hole is dug in the ground, a wooden fire is lit in the hole and the cooks wait for embers to form. The whole lamb is threaded onto a spit and balanced on forked poles that have been placed on either side of the pit. The lamb is then cooked for about 6 hours, basted from time to time with melted, salted butter. For those unsure about digging up their garden, this dish can be rotisserie grilled or roasted in a conventional oven.

1 leg of lamb, approximately 5 lb/2^1/$_4$ kg
5 tablespoons butter, melted
3 cloves garlic, peeled and crushed
2 tablespoons kosher or sea salt
2 tablespoons freshly ground black pepper
2 tablespoons ground cumin
1 tablespoon ground coriander
1 teaspoon paprika

1 Preheat the oven or rotisserie grill to 400°F (200°C). Combine the melted butter, garlic, 1 teaspoon each of salt, pepper and cumin, the coriander and the paprika. Rub the lamb with the seasoned butter.
2 If using a rotisserie, skewer the lamb and attach it to the turnspit over the grill. Alternatively, place the lamb in a large roasting pan and place it on the top rack of the oven. Grill or bake for 30 minutes then reduce the heat to 300°F (150°C) and grill or roast for 3 hours, basting regularly with the juices. The meat is done when the outside is dark brown and crispy, and the internal temperature is about 170°F (80°C). Remove the lamb from heat and set it aside to rest for 15 minutes.
3 Fill three small bowls with the remaining salt, pepper and cumin. Carve the lamb into large pieces and serve it with the spices. Roasted Spiced Eggplant Puree and Roasted Bell Peppers are good accompaniments (page 39).

Serves 12   Preparation time: 20 mins   Cooking time: 3^1/$_2$ hours

Veal with Crisp-fried Cauliflower

2 teaspoons salt
1 head firm cauliflower, broken into florets
3 tablespoons olive oil
2$^{1}/_{2}$ lbs (1$^{1}/_{4}$ kg) boneless veal, cubed
1 onion, peeled and thinly sliced
1 teaspoon salt
2 teaspoons freshly ground black pepper
$^{1}/_{2}$ teaspoon saffron threads
2 bay leaves
2 cups (500 ml) water
3 eggs
2 cloves garlic, peeled and crushed
1 cup (150 g) flour
Oil for deep-frying

1 Blanch the cauliflower in salted boiling water for 5 minutes, drain and set aside.
2 In a large pot, combine the olive oil, veal, onion, salt, 1 teaspoon of the black pepper, the saffron, bay leaves, and water. Bring to a boil over high heat, taste, and adjust the seasoning. Cover, reduce the heat to low and simmer for 45 minutes.
3 Break the eggs into a mixing bowl and beat them lightly. Add the remaining teaspoon of pepper and the garlic, mix well, and set aside. Put the flour on a plate and set it next to the egg mixture.
4 Heat the oil in a pan. Take a cauliflower floret, dip first in the egg mixture, then in the flour, then fry in the oil, ensuring that each piece is evenly browned, about 5–7 minutes. Remove and drain on paper towels. Repeat with the remaining cauliflower. Remove the veal from the heat. Transfer it to a serving dish and arrange the fried cauliflower on top.

Serves 4   Preparation time: 45 mins   Cooking time: 1$^{1}/_{2}$ hours

Meatball Tagine with Eggs

1³/₄ lbs (800 g) ground beef or veal
1 large onion, peeled and diced
1 bunch fresh coriander leaves (cilantro), chopped
1 teaspoon salt
¹/₂ teaspoon freshly ground black pepper
1 teaspoon paprika
5 tablespoons olive oil
One 12-oz (350 g) can peeled, chopped tomatoes
6 eggs

1 Combine the ground meat, onion, chopped coriander leaves, salt, pepper, and paprika in a bowl. Rinse your hands in cold water, then gather a bit of the mixture into your hands and roll it into a ball. Moisten your hands with water before rolling each meatball.
2 Heat the oil in a tagine or other earthenware dish and sauté the meatballs over medium–high heat for 15 minutes. Halfway through cooking the meatballs, add the tomato and mix well.
3 Break the eggs over the meatballs, cover the tagine and cook for 3 minutes or until the eggs are cooked. Serve hot.

Serves 4   Preparation time: 30 mins   Cooking time: 20 mins

Fish with Mixed Vegetables and Couscous

3 tablespoons oil
2 onions, peeled and sliced
2 cloves garlic, peeled and crushed
1 small globe eggplants
2 carrots, peeled and cut in half
1 turnip, peeled and cut in half
1 medium-sized summer squash, cut in half
2 medium-sized tomatoes, peeled and diced
$^1/_2$ lemon
1 teaspoon ground cumin
1 bunch fresh coriander leaves (cilantro)
4 cups (1 liter) water, lightly salted
$2^1/_2$ lbs ($1^1/_2$ kg) cod or sea bass fillets, cut into 6 pieces or 3 whole fish (like
  sea bream), scaled, gutted, and rinsed clean
Pinch of salt
1 portion prepared Couscous (page 34)
$^1/_2$ teaspoon ground saffron

1 Place the oil, onions, garlic and vegetables in a pot. Add the lemon, cumin, coriander leaves, and salted water. Cover and cook over medium heat for 25 minutes. Drop the fish into the stock, cook for 10 minutes, then remove and set it aside. Bring the stock back to a boil, add the salt, and remove and discard the coriander leaves.
2 While the vegetables are cooking, make the Couscous as instructed on page 34, adding the saffron to color and flavor the grains.
3 Serve the fish on a bed of couscous, surrounded by the vegetables. Ladle a little stock over the dish and serve extra stock on the side.

Serves 6   Preparation time: 30 mins   Cooking time: 35 mins

Fish with Olives and Bell Peppers

3 tablespoons olive oil
3 lbs (1$^1/_2$ kg) cod, pollack or any flaky white fish fillets, cut into large pieces
3 medium-sized tomatoes, peeled and sliced
1 green bell pepper, cut in rings
3 cloves garlic, peeled and crushed
1 Preserved Lemon (page 35), cut in wedges or $^1/_2$ fresh lemon
1 cup (250 g) mixed green and black olives
$^1/_2$ teaspoon freshly ground black pepper
$^1/_2$ teaspoon ground cumin
2 cups (500 ml) water

Garnishes
1 small bunch flat-leaf parsley, chopped
1 small bunch fresh coriander leaves (cilantro), chopped

1 In an earthenware tagine or large cast-iron pan, heat the oil and add the pieces of fish, tomato, bell pepper, garlic, Preserved Lemon (or fresh lemon), olives, pepper, cumin and water. Simmer, covered, over low heat for 45 minutes if using a tagine, 35 minutes if using a pot.
2 Serve garnished with the chopped parsley and coriander leaves.

Serves 6   Preparation time: 30 mins   Cooking time: 45 mins

Baked Stuffed Sardines

Try to find the smaller, less oily, Mediterranean sardines for this dish.

2 lbs (1 kg) fresh sardines, boned and butterflied by the fishmonger
2 tablespoons olive oil
$^1/_2$ lemon, thinly sliced
$^1/_2$ teaspoon salt
$^1/_2$ teaspoon ground turmeric
$^1/_2$ teaspoon ground cumin
$^1/_4$ teaspoon ground white pepper
One 12-oz (350-g) can peeled, chopped tomatoes
2 cloves garlic, peeled and crushed
4 tablespoons water
$^3/_4$ cup (100 g) olives

Stuffing
1 small bunch fresh coriander leaves (cilantro), chopped
1 small bunch flat-leaf parsley, chopped
2 cloves garlic, peeled and crushed
Juice of $^1/_2$ lemon
1 tablespoon uncooked rice
$^1/_2$ teaspoon salt
$^1/_2$ teaspoon ground turmeric
$^1/_2$ teaspoon ground cumin
$^1/_4$ teaspoon ground white pepper
2 tablespoons olive oil

1 To prepare the Stuffing, combine the chopped coriander leaves, parsley, garlic, lemon juice, rice, salt, turmeric, cumin, pepper, and oil. Mix well and set aside.
2 Dry the sardines with paper towels. Lay one fish skin side down and spread a tablespoon of Stuffing over the flesh. Cover with the second sardine and set aside. Repeat with the remaining sardines.
3 Preheat the oven to 400°F (200°C). Line a baking sheet with parchment paper and brush it with the olive oil. Scatter the lemon slices, salt, spices, tomatoes, and garlic on the lined sheet and top with the stuffed sardines. Bake for 20 minutes. Serve with the baked lemon slices and olives.

Serves 4   Preparation time: 1 hour   Cooking time: 20 mins

Baked Fish Stuffed with Almonds and Dates

1 whole fish (such as tilapia), about
  3 lbs/1^1/$_2$ kg, cleaned and scaled
^{1}/$_2$ lemon
1 teaspoon salt

Stuffing
^{1}/$_2$ cup (125 g) butter
2 large onions, peeled and diced,
10 fresh dates, pitted
1^1/$_4$ cups (310 g) blanched and
  peeled almonds, sautéed in oil until
  golden
^{1}/$_2$ teaspoon ground nutmeg
^{1}/$_2$ teaspoon ground saffron
Pinch of salt
^{1}/$_2$ teaspoon freshly ground black
  pepper
1 tablespoon orange flower water
  (page 32)

1 Rub the fish with the lemon, juicing it as you go. Then rub the fish with the salt and set it aside.

2 To prepare the Stuffing, melt 2 tablespoons of the butter in a skillet over low heat and sauté the onion until golden. Set aside to cool. Grind the dates and almonds and the remaining butter together in a food processor. Combine the ground dates and almonds with the sautéed onion, spices, salt, pepper, orange flower water and a few more drops of lemon juice in a bowl and mix well.

3 Preheat the oven to 425°F (220°C). Fill the fish two-thirds full of Stuffing and sew it shut. Place the fish into a greased baking dish.

4 Roll any leftover Stuffing into little balls and place them around the fish. Bake for 30 minutes and serve immediately.

Serves 4   Preparation time: 30 mins   Cooking time: 40 mins

Almond Pastry Snake

Almond Paste
2 cups (500 g) blanched and peeled almonds
$^2/_3$ cup (150 g) sugar
1 teaspoon ground cinnamon
2 tablespoons orange flower water (page 32)
$^3/_4$ cup (180 g) butter, softened

Pastry
8 sheets filo pastry or Warka Pastry Leaf (page 35)
1 egg white, lightly beaten
$^1/_2$ cup (120 g) butter, melted

$^1/_4$ cup (60 ml) honey, warmed
$^1/_2$ teaspoon ground cinnamon

1 Prepare the Almond Paste by grinding the almonds and the sugar in a
food processor. Add the cinnamon, orange flower water, and butter and
process until the paste holds its shape in a ball. Roll the paste into 4 long
snake-like rolls, a little bit shorter than the length of a sheet of pastry, and
set them aside.
2 Preheat the oven to 400°F (200° C). Lay one sheet of pastry on a clean
surface and brush it with melted butter. Lay a second sheet of pastry on top
of the first one and brush it with butter. Place one roll of Almond Paste on
the edge of the pastry and roll it up, tucking the ends in to enclose the filling. Repeat with the remaining sheets of pastry and Almond Paste rolls.
3 Grease a round baking dish. Tightly coil one pastry roll and place it in the
center of the dish. Add the remaining pastry rolls to the dish, forming a
large spiral. Brush the pastry with the remaining melted butter and bake for
30 minutes or until golden. Serve drizzled with warm honey and dusted with
ground cinnamon.

Serves 6   Preparation time: 45 mins   Cooking time: 10 mins

Sweet Egg Custard Pastries

8 sheets filo pastry or Warka Pastry
  Leaf (page 35)
5 tablespoons butter, melted
10 dates
18 shelled walnut halves

Egg Custard
4 cups (1 liter) milk
1¹/₂ cup (375 g) sugar
2 eggs, beaten
3 tablespoons orange flower or rosewater (page 32)

1 Make the Custard by bringing the milk just to a boil in a saucepan, then add the sugar and mix well. Remove from heat and add the eggs, whisking thoroughly. Return to the heat, stirring constantly. Remove from heat as soon as the custard boils and add the orange flower or rosewater. Set aside to cool.

2 Paste two sheets of filo together with a little melted butter in between. Add a little of the melted butter to a skillet and toast the double layer of pastry until golden on both sides. Assemble and toast the remaining sheets of pastry in the same manner.

3 To serve, place one toasted pastry sheet on a dish and spread a layer of Custard over the top. Alternate layers of pastry and Custard and garnish with dates and walnuts on top.

Serves 4   Preparation time: 30 mins   Cooking time: 40 mins

Crunchy Almond Pastries

2 tablespoons oil
2 cups (500 g) blanched and peeled
  almonds
1 cup (250 g) sugar
12 sheets filo pastry or Warka Pastry
  Leaf (page 35)
5 tablespoons butter
2 cups (500 ml) milk
¹/₂ tablespoon orange flower water

1 Heat the oil over medium heat in a skillet. Fry the almonds until golden and drain on paper towels. Chop the almonds, combine them with the sugar and set aside.

2 Prepare the pastry sheets according to Step 2 in the recipe for Sweet Egg Custard Pastries above. To assemble, place a toasted filo sheet on a dish and sprinkle with the almond/sugar mixture. Continue stacking, alternating layers, and finishing with a layer of pastry.

3 Warm the milk and add the orange flower water. Pour the warm milk over the stack and serve.

Serves 4   Preparation time: 30 mins   Cooking time: 10 mins

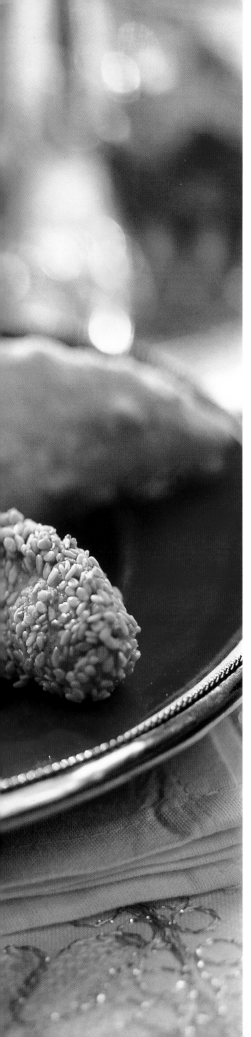

Almond Crescents

Almond Paste
3 cups (450 g) blanched and peeled almonds
1 cup (150 g) sugar
$1/2$ teaspoon ground cinnamon
1 tablespoon orange flower water (page 32)
1 egg white, lightly beaten
3 tablespoons butter, melted

Pastry Dough
$1/2$ tablespoon melted butter
$1 2/3$ cups (250 g) flour
$1/4$ cup (60 ml) orange flower water (page 32)

$1/4$ cup (60 g) butter, melted
Confectioners' sugar, for dusting

1 To make the Almond Paste, grind the almonds and the sugar to a fine powder in a food processor. Add the orange flower water and the melted butter and mix well. Separate the mixture into small pieces and roll into batons about $1 1/4$ in x $1/2$ in (3 cm x 1 cm). Set aside.
2 Mix all the ingredients for the Pastry Dough together. Roll the Dough as thin as possible with a rolling pin. It should be almost transparent. Place the batons of almond paste on the dough in a line with even spaces between each. Fold the Dough over the Almond Paste to cover all the pieces. Seal it by pressing slightly and separate them using a sharp knife or a pastry cutter. Bend each piece slightly to form a crescent.
3 Preheat the oven to 400°F (200°C). Prick each cresent with a pin to allow the steam to escape during baking. Transfer to a greased baking sheet, brush with melted butter, then bake in the oven for 10 minutes or until the crescents are barely golden. Serve plain or dusted with confectioners' sugar.

Note: For less experienced pastry chefs, you can replace the dough with $1 1/2$ cups (180 g) toasted sesame seeds. Beat two eggs in a bowl, dip the batons of almond paste first in the egg, then in the seeds, shape into crescents, and bake for 7 minutes at 400°F (200°C).

Makes 30 pastries   Preparation time: $1 1/2$ hours   Baking time: 20 mins

Sweet Almond Triangles

12 sheets filo pastry or Warka Pastry
  Leaf (page 35)
Oil for deep-frying
1 cup (250 g) honey, warmed
Toasted sesame seeds for garnishing

Almond Paste
2 cups (300 g) blanched and peeled
  almonds
$1/_2$ cup (125 g) sugar
1 teaspoon ground cinnamon
1 tablespoon orange flower water
  (page 32)
1 tablespoon butter, melted

1 To make the Almond Paste, grind the almonds to a fine powder in a food processor. Mix the ground almonds with the sugar, cinnamon, orange flower water and butter and set aside.
2 Cut each pastry sheets into 4 strips, place a spoonful of filling at one end, fold over the corner to make a triangle, then continue folding at right angles. To seal, tuck in the opposite end like an envelope (page 35).
3 Heat the oil in a pan over medium–high heat. Fry the triangles until golden and drain on paper towels. Roll each pastry in a dish of warm honey, sprinkle with sesame seeds and serve.

Makes 40   Preparation time: $1^1/_2$ hours   Cooking time: 30 mins

Sweet Almond Cigars

12 sheets filo pastry or Waarka
  (page 35)
1 egg, lightly beaten
Oil for deep-frying
1 cup (250 ml) honey
Toasted sesame seeds, for ganishing

Almond Paste
2 cups (300 g) blanched and peeled
  almonds
$1/_2$ cup (125 g) sugar
1 teaspoon ground cinnamon
1 tablespoon orange flower water
1 tablespoon butter, melted

1 To make the Almond Paste, grind the almonds to a fine powder in a food processor. Mix the ground almonds with the sugar, cinnamon, orange flower water and butter and knead into a ball. Separate into small pieces and roll each piece into a stick $2^1/_2$–3 in (6–7 cm) long.
2 Cut the pastry sheets in half, place a stick of Almond Paste along one short edge, fold in the two sides, then roll up like a cigar. Seal with beaten egg.
3 Heat the oil in a pan over medium–high heat. Fry the cigars until golden and drain on paper towels. Roll each fried pastry in a dish of warm honey then roll each end in toasted sesame seeds. Repeat with the rest of the pastries.

Makes 24 pastries   Preparation time:$1^1/_2$ hours   Cooking time: 30 mins

Cinnamon Rice Pudding

$^{1}/_{2}$ cup (200 g) uncooked short-grain rice

$^{1}/_{2}$ cup (125 ml) water

Pinch of salt

4 cups (1 liter) milk

1 cinnamon stick

$^{1}/_{4}$ cup (60 g) sugar

$^{3}/_{8}$ cup (100 g) blanched and peeled almonds

1 tablespoon oil

1 teaspoon cinnamon

1 teaspoon confectioners' sugar

1 Combine the rice, water and salt in a heavy saucepan. Bring to a boil, reduce the heat and simmer for 5 minutes or until most of the water has been absorbed.

2 Add 1 cup (250 ml) of milk, the cinnamon stick and the sugar to the rice and bring to a simmer. Cook until the liquid has been absorbed. Add another cup (250 ml) of milk and repeat until all the milk has been absorbed into the rice. Discard the cinnamon stick and set aside to cool.

3 Heat the oil in a skillet over medium heat and fry the almonds until golden. Chop half of the almonds.

4 Serve the pudding sprinkled with cinnamon and sugar and garnish with chopped and whole almonds.

Serves 4   Preparation time: 30 mins   Cooking time: 1$^{1}/_{2}$ hours

Honey Wheat Pudding

2 cups (250 g) whole grain wheat
4 cups (1 liter) water
2 teaspoons salt
4 cups (1 liter) milk
1 tablespoon sugar
1 tablespoon orange flower water
  (page 32)
4 tablespoons honey

1 Soak the wheat in 2 cups (500 ml) water with $1^1/_2$ teaspoons salt for 1 hour.
2 Drain the wheat, then bring it to a boil in 2 cups (500 ml) water with $^1/_2$ teaspoon salt, and simmer for 35 minutes. Drain again.
3 Bring the milk to a boil and add the wheat, sugar and orange flower water. Simmer for an additional 10 minutes. Drizzle with honey and serve hot.

Serves 4   Preparation time: 20 mins + 1 hour to soak   Cooking time: 45 mins

Green Mint Tea

The more mint you use, the more fragrant the tea will be.

4 cups (1 liter) water
1 teaspoon Gunpowder tea or other Chinese green tea
4–6 lumps of sugar
1 bunch fresh mint, washed and patted dry

1 Boil the water. Put the tea in a small teapot. Add 1 or 2 glasses of boiling water, then discard the water, making sure to leave the tea leaves in the pot. Add the mint to the teapot and fill it with boiling water. Add the sugar.
2 To serve, pour out a glass of tea. Pour the contents of the glass back into the teapot and repeat 3 or 4 times until the ingredients are completely mixed. Serve.

Serves 4   Preparation time: 10 mins

Traditional Almond Milk

2 cups (300 g) blanched and peeled
  almonds
4 cups (1 liter) water
1 cup (250 g) superfine sugar
1 teaspoon orange flower water
  (page 32—optional)

1 Grind the almonds in a food processor. Add the water and process thoroughly. Line a strainer with cheesecloth and place it over a bowl. Strain the almond mixture, pressing on the solids to extract as much "milk" as possible. Add the sugar and the orange flower water and chill in the refrigerator before serving.

Serves 4   Preparation time: 45 mins   Cooking time: 5 mins

Enriched Almond Milk

2 cups (300 g) blanched and peeled
  almonds
4 cups (1 liter) low-fat milk
1¼ cups (310 g) superfine sugar
1 teaspoon orange flower water
  (page 32—optional)

1 Prepare according to the instructions in the previous recipe but instead of water, use milk.

Serves 4   Preparation time: 45 mins   Cooking time: 5 mins

Complete list of recipes

Measurements and conversions

Measurements in this book are given in volume as far as possible. Teaspoon, tablespoon and cup measurements should be level, not heaped, unless otherwise indicated. Australian readers please note that the standard Australian measuring spoon is larger than the UK or American spoon by 5 ml, so use $3/4$ tablespoon instead of a full tablespoon when following the recipes.

Liquid Conversions

Imperial	Metric	US cups
$1/2$ fl oz	15 ml	1 tablespoon
1 fl oz	30 ml	$1/8$ cup
2 fl oz	60 ml	$1/4$ cup
3 fl oz	85 ml	$1/3$ cup
4 fl oz	125 ml	$1/2$ cup
5 fl oz	150 ml	$2/3$ cup
6 fl oz	175 ml	$3/4$ cup
8 fl oz	250 ml	1 cup
12 fl oz	375 ml	$1^1/2$ cups
16 fl oz	500 ml	2 cups
1 quart	1 liter	4 cups

Note: 1 UK pint = 20 fl oz
        1 US pint = 16 fl oz

Solid Weight Conversions

Imperial	Metric
$1/2$ oz	15 g
1 oz	28 g
$1^1/2$ oz	45 g
2 oz	60 g
3 oz	85 g
$3^1/2$ oz	100 g
4 oz ($1/4$ lb)	125 g
5 oz	150 g
6 oz	175 g
7 oz	200 g
8 oz	250 g
9 oz	260 g
10 oz	300 g
16 oz (1 lb)	500 g
32 oz (2 lbs)	1 kg

Oven Temperatures

Heat	Fahrenheit	Centigrade/Celsius	British Gas Mark
Very cool	230	110	$1/4$
Cool or slow	275–300	135–150	1–2
Moderate	350	175	4
Hot	425	220	7
Very hot	450	230	8